## World University Library

The World University Library is an international series
of books, each of which has been specially commissioned.
The authors are leading scientists and scholars from all over
the world who, in an age of increasing specialisation, see the
need for a broad, up-to-date presentation of their subject.
The aim is to provide authoritative introductory books for
university students which will be of interest also to the general
reader. The series is published in Britain, France, Germany,
Holland, Italy, Spain, Sweden and the United States.

# Contents

Foreword 7

1 The geological framework 9

2 Methods of dating and study 15

3 Africa – the cradle of mankind ? 32

4 The Abbevillian and Acheulean
developments in Europe 51

5 The Acheulean in Africa 64

6 The Acheulean in Asia 77

7 Lower Palaeolithic industries
without handaxes 83

8 The Mousterian stage in Europe 98

9 The Mousterian stage in Africa 121

10 The Mousterian stage in Asia 126

11 A general review of the Old
and Middle Palaeolithic 131

12 The Upper Palaeolithic in France 147

13 The Upper Palaeolithic in western
and central Europe 167

14 The Upper Palaeolithic in eastern Europe 183

15 The Upper Palaeolithic in Asia 198

16 The Upper Palaeolithic in Africa 204

17 Japan, various islands and Australia 210

18 The Palaeolithic in America 213

19 A general review of the Upper
Palaeolithic period 220

Glossary 242

Bibliography 250

# Acknowledgments

Acknowledgment – further to any made in the captions – is due to the following for illustrations (the number refers to the page on which the illustration appears); 20, 67, 114–5, 142–3, 233, Author; 43, 66, 70, 71, 141, F. Clark Howell; 56, 57, 94, British Museum (Natural History); 80, Professors Von Koenigswald and Movius; 87, American Museum of Natural History; 90–1, Dr L. Vértes; 148–9, 236, Professor Leroi-Gourhan; 165, 237, Alain Roussot; 174–5, Moravian National Museum, Brno; 181, Dr Joseph Karáth.

The line drawings were made by Pierre Laurent and are the copyright of the publishers. The maps and section drawings were prepared by Design Practitioners Limited. Acknowledgment is due to Professor Desmond Clark and Penguin Books Limited for the section drawing on page 74, which appeared in *Prehistory of Southern Africa*.

# Foreword

The peasants of Périgord have a curious expression for archaeologists: they call them the people who are looking for 'the savage
Christian souls', or – more naively still for 'the Christian souls
before the time of Christ'. The word 'Christian' here simply means
'men'; and this expression has always seemed to me to express the
continuity of the human race, whose childhood can be considered
as coinciding with the Palaeolithic period. The childhood years are
of supreme importance; and recently it has even been maintained
that our aggressive tendencies are inherited from our first ancestors
who made the transition from frugivores to carnivores.

It is not easy within the compass of two hundred pages to give a
complete and accurate picture of the tremendous epic of primitive
man, and this will therefore not be attempted. We shall simply try
to indicate the main lines along which the Palaeolithic period
developed throughout the world. We shall try to set out the facts;
but scientific facts are always more or less coloured by interpretation, and each man's mind acts like a lens, which concentrates the
rays according to its focus. It is only right to warn that not everything set down here will always have the approval of our colleagues.
There are a variety of schools in the field of prehistory. In France,
the emphasis is especially on stratigraphy and typology; in the
English-speaking countries, on the relationship between man and
his environment; in the USSR, on palaeo-sociology. Of course,
things are not quite as simple as this, and French researchers do not
neglect the findings of ecology and sociology, any more than
Americans or Russians neglect stratigraphy; it is more a question of
stressing one point of view or another.

There are historical reasons for this tendency. In France, the first
study of prehistory was the work of naturalists. The Americans
however, with primitive peoples still living among them, were able
to study their relationship with the environment. The Soviet
interest in palaeo-sociology comes partly from their Marxist out-

look. But even at this stage we must modify these statements by adding 'as a general rule', or 'perhaps', as we shall be forced to do throughout this book. Although prehistory has now been accepted as a science, it is not yet – and will surely never be – an exact science. Mathematical methods (such as the statistical analysis of industries), or physical methods (such as dating by means of radioactive carbon or the potassium-argon method), have certainly contributed a great deal to our researches; but there still exists a wide field in which we must confess ignorance. There have been finds – though few and far between – which show that Palaeolithic man used wood; but in a general way we cannot say anything about the use he made of it. We mostly can only make deductions. For instance, the existence of numerous bone needles in the Magda-lenian period is very likely evidence of clothing that was stitched together. But the absence of needles would be no proof that men before this time went about naked; for clothes can be put together without needles.

In this book we are going to look at the evolution of the Palaeo-lithic age, that is to say the evolution of cultures, for the physical evolution of man is no part of our purpose. But it is difficult to present a play without introducing the actors, so we shall say a word or two about them, as far as anything is known. Paradoxically enough, we now have better knowledge about the men of the most ancient Palaeolithic period than of their successors. Continuing with our analogy from the theatre, we might say that whereas there are plenty of characters in the first act, there are very few in the second, and the stage is practically empty in the third. It begins to fill up again, however, in the fourth and fifth acts. But before we come to the play itself, it will be as well to look at the setting.

# 1 The geological framework

The human span is very brief as compared with the age of the earth, which the most recent estimates put at certainly not less than four or five thousand million years. The Tertiary era – the so-called era of the mammals, though they in fact made their appearance earlier – saw them branch out into a multitude of forms, amongst which were the primates. At the end of the Tertiary, in the final Pliocene period the stage was ready for the appearance of man, not as we know him today but in ancestral forms. Incidentally, it is difficult to decide at what precise moment a being can be considered human. Today there is a tendency to draw the dividing line at the ability to *make* tools – with the accent on the word 'make', for the anthropoid apes seem to some extent capable of *using* rudimentary tools (such as sticks for reaching fruit), and even of improving them (by fitting one bamboo into another). The earliest known fabricated tools date from the Upper Villafranchian period, that is to say, from the end of the first division of the Quaternary. Until quite recently, the highest estimate put the length of the Quaternary period at about a million years. But the latest dating arrived at by the potassium-argon method has pushed this line back considerably, so that the earliest tools, not falling within the beginning of the Quaternary Period, would go back about 1,900,000 years. These were found in the Olduvai deposits in East Africa.

During this long span of time, the earth's face has undergone various transformations, and although the continents had been formed long before, there are many details that have only taken shape since that period. The great river valleys had by no means reached their present depth. In Africa, the interplay of groups of faults (in the strata) in the region of the Great Lakes brought about great changes which had their effect on human life. Above all, marked variations in the climate of the temperate zones during the glacial and interglacial periods brought about notable variations in the flora and fauna. In the course of the Pleistocene period great sheets of ice of tremendous thickness formed several times over the northern mountains of Europe and America, and moved down towards the south. Other less extensive glaciers existed in all the high mountains, and those which covered the Alps extended as far as Lyons in France. It is to be noted that the greatest degree of cold did not always, it seems, coincide with the greatest extension of these ice-fields (figure 1).

Between the ice-ages there were periods of temperate or even warm climate, the interglacial periods. And even within the ice-ages, there were less marked or shorter climatic variations, the inter-stadial periods, which may well have brought about a more moderate climate.

In the temperate latitudes, the chronological framework is generally provided by the ice-ages. There were at least four of these in Europe, known respectively as the Günz, Mindel, Riss and Würm ice-ages, passing from the most ancient to the most recent, and named after tributaries of the Danube. But there were probably still more ancient ice-ages, which it has been proposed to call the Biber and the Danube. In the United States, the nomenclature is different. It is difficult to give exact dates – or even cautious approximations – for these ice-ages. The last of them would seem to have come to an end about 9,000 years before our era, and would appear to have begun some 75 to 90,000 years before our era. The Riss ice-age must have been about 200,000 years before our era, but it was a very lengthy period, interrupted by strong periodic recessions. The Mindel ice-age is sometimes dated about 500,000 years ago.

We naturally know more about the recent ice-ages than about the older ones. We are beginning to get a fairly detailed picture of the Würm ice-age. In France, it is often thought to have consisted of four main stages, with secondary fluctuations. In central Europe, the tendency is to restrict this to three stages, the first of which includes the first two French stages.

In lower latitudes, we are without the indications given by the ice-ages, with their moraines and their covering of loess. It is thought that there are indications of rainy periods, when the rainfall was much greater than in our times. But this is at present a much debated point; and in any case the correlation between the rainy periods and the ice-ages (were they contemporary, or alternating?) is far from clear. This is the reason why the time-scale for Africa and Asia – apart from the Himalayan region – has been less fully worked out than for Europe.

Although the glaciers themselves have sometimes served as barriers, it is the periglacial phenomena – in the widest sense – that exercised the greatest influence on the life of palaeolithic man. Throughout a wide zone surrounding the glaciers, the phenomena connected with solifluction made themselves felt. The soil would freeze to a great depth, and when a thaw set in, the water – unable to filter through – caused the upper layers of the soil to run down over the bare slopes in the form of liquid mud, carrying with it the remains of human settlements and probably making hunting extremely difficult. During the periods of dry cold climates, fine dust, carried along by the wind, would settle over a wide area – the so-called loess, which has sealed and protected the open-air sites. At the entrance to caves and under rock shelters, the cold would cause the rocks to split and break off larger or smaller fragments which would fall on to the ground and become blended with the remains of human activity, thus constituting the layers studied by archaeology. During the more temperate periods, these deposits were small and occasional, and soil would be built up through the agency of vegetation; so in caves and rock shelters, there would be less rocky deposits and the layers would have more soil in them. It is thus possible, by the pedological study of soils and the sedimentological study of sheltered places, also by the study of the flora

*Figure 1* Maximal extension of the glaciers over Europe. A large part of Britain is covered by them while Central Europe forms a narrow corridor.

(pollens) and fauna, to reconstruct the climatic variations that have taken place (figures 2 and 3).

Throughout the Quaternary period, there were variations in the flora and fauna, brought about by the extinction or shifting of species, or by the alternation of arctic or warm flora and fauna in the present-day temperate regions. These changes were not perceptible at the very beginning of an ice-age. In south-western France for instance, at the beginning of the Würm age, the fauna was still temperate in type and there were only a very few reindeer. Reindeer were very late in reaching Italy and hardly penetrated at all into Spain.

To get a picture of western Europe during the Würm age, we should not make a close comparison with Lapland or Alaska, for Europe has never known the Arctic polar nights or oblique sun which result from the difference in latitude. There has always been a more abundant fauna and a richer vegetation so that Europe has always been able to carry a greater density of hunting peoples than is possible in the arctic zone.

# 2 Methods of dating and study

The first datings were made by means of stratigraphy and palae-ontology, for the first pre-historians were either naturalists or amateurs trained in natural history. But one need have no hesitation in saying that even today stratigraphy remains, and must remain, the very basis of chronological study.

Boucher de Perthes (1788–1868) and his contemporaries had shown, as early as 1850–60, that man had lived at the same time as animal species that had disappeared at a very early period. The find made by Lartet and Christy in the shelter of Madeleine (in the Dordogne) of a drawing of a mammoth on a fragment of mam-moth tusk may be said to have given a double proof that man was contemporary with the mammoth. This led to the recognition of different epochs from their fauna and the nature of the chipped flints; but although it was noticed in certain deposits that these epochs lay superimposed upon one another, there was no question in the early days of arriving at any very accurate stratigraphy. In spite of the pioneer work of Victor Brun, who was able (as early as 1860) to distinguish at Bruniquel (Tarn) levels only five to ten centimetres in thickness, it was only later that people began to realise the value of distinguishing the possible variations of the fauna and of man's industries within one and the same epoch.

Nowadays, in well-managed excavations, stratigraphy plays a part quite unknown to the early explorers. It is not only a question today of distinguishing the often obvious geological strata, but also of determining the archaeological levels. In the same red sand or the same calcareous debris there may be, and often are, several archaeological levels, and there is no *a priori* guarantee that they all belong to the same culture: they may well have to be separated. And even if one is dealing in a general way with the same industry, it is necessary to make subdivisions in order to trace its development. The days are past when it was enough to write: 'the Mousterian layer is a metre [or several metres!] in depth'.

Methods of excavation vary according to the problems to be solved and even the nature of the deposits to be excavated. The old method of vertical trench-excavation should no longer be used except for limited probing. But a modified form of it is necessary when the stratigraphy is difficult. In such a case one excavates in cubic metres, a cube at a time, so that there is always a vertical section ready to hand as a check. Of course, the vertical and horizontal positions of any objects found are noted, and if a structure is encountered, the surface of excavation is enlarged. In deposits where the layers are very distinct, horizontal excavation is convenient, for it enables one to photograph or make drawings of the occupation level and to distinguish more readily the palae-ethnographic data (such as hearths, stake-holes, hut-floors, etc.). But it may be very dangerous if applied to deposits where the stratigraphy is difficult, and where it is easy to pass from one level to another without being aware of it. This is apt to make one suppose that objects are arranged in a particular horizontal pattern, when this is in fact a pure illusion. In the case of thick layers made up of lenses of different deposits it is also dangerous; for one is apt to isolate artificial 'floors', and there is a temptation to draw conclusions about the relative position of objects which may well be separated by decades or centuries. In excavating, one must always keep an open mind and adopt the method particularly suitable for the moment or the problem in hand.

The archaeological method has often been used, on the assumption that in a particular geographical zone identical or very similar industries have a strong chance of being contemporary. But the opposite is often the case, and we shall come across different but contemporary industries in the same region. This archeological method suffered some striking reverses in its early days when an attempt was made to extend the French sequence to the world as a whole, and to talk for instance of the Magdalenian in India. When

*Figure 2* Schematic section through the loesses.
A, solifluction pebble band; B, interglacial soil;
B1, postglacial soil; b, interstadial soils.
The section bears upon the three Rissian
loesses and the three Würmian loesses.

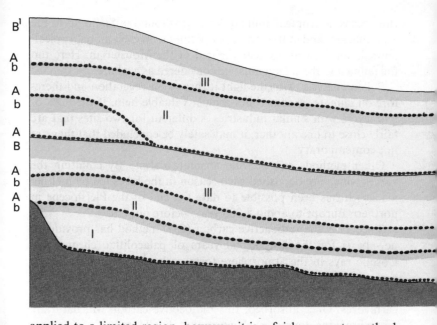

applied to a limited region, however, it is a fairly accurate method if industries as a whole are considered, and not simply one or two implements that are taken to be characteristic. For once a type or a technique has been discovered, it is rarely abandoned altogether: there are usually some recurring examples.

The palaeontological method was one of the first to find favour, and in 1858 Lartet was thus able to distinguish between the Great Bear age, the Elephant and Rhinoceros Age, the Reindeer Age and the Auroch Age. But things are clearly not as simple as this, for fauna can recur, and – what is more serious – a particular animal form may survive in certain places. Thus at Krapina in Yugoslavia, where a Mousterian site had been found, it was judged to belong to the last Interglacial because remains were found of Merck's rhinoceros, a 'tropical' animal. Well, it is found in Spain up to the Aurignacian; and in Italy the hippopotamus, an even more 'tropical' animal, survived up to near the end of the Mousterian. Here too the fauna and the region must be considered as a whole.

Pollen analysis, with the light it throws on vegetation and therefore on climate, is sometimes a most valuable help. If the flora of two layers with similar industries is different for two sites that are fairly close to one another, it may safely be concluded that they are not contemporary.

Other methods can provide absolute dating. By counting the varves which are deposited each season in the lakes fed by melting glaciers it has been possible to date the end of the Pleistocene in northern Europe to about 8,000 years before our era.

Since 1949 the radioactive carbon ($C^{14}$) method has provided a new basis for the last 60,000 years of palaeolithic chronology. Cosmic rays in the atmosphere form carbon$^{14}$, an isotope of the carbon$^{12}$. Part of this radioactive carbon is absorbed by plants and so passes into the bodies of the herbivores and thence to the carnivores. Once absorbed, this radioactive carbon will naturally go on breaking down in such a way that it will lose half of its atoms every 5,730 years. As there are good reasons to suppose that living creatures absorb this radioactive carbon at a practically constant rate, it is thus possible to determine the date when an organism died and hence the age of the layer in which it was found. However, below a certain proportion of $C^{14}$, errors of measurement become so great that the method can no longer be used. The extreme limit – making use of isotopic enrichment – has been extended to 60 or 70,000 years; but there is then no very high degree of accuracy.

Errors may also arise for other reasons. In the first place, because atoms of $C^{14}$ break down in haphazard and not in uniform fashion. The dates given by laboratories express this as a standard deviation: for example, a date would be given not as 15,300 years but as 15,300 ± 300. This notation has often been imperfectly understood. It means that there is a sixty-seven per cent chance of the correct figure falling between 15,000 and 15,600; but it does not mean that the correct figure *must* lie between these two extremes. The chances rise to ninety-six per cent if one accepts a possible double margin of error. Now this margin, though insignificant when applied to the Middle Palaeolithic, becomes very important when one is dealing with the Upper Palaeolithic, and may for instance altogether reverse the supposed direction of a migration. This statistical error may be reduced by increasing the time spent on these measurements, but it cannot be altogether eliminated.

There are also other causes of error. In the past, the rate of formation of $C^{14}$ may have fluctuated – though not, it seems, to any great extent. The different materials (charcoal, peat, charred or uncharred bones) do not always yield the same dates, for certain specimens have been contaminated by more recent organic matter (resulting in rather too low figures). When shells are measured by this test the dates given are often too high, for molluscs absorb ancient carbonates. The ages thus arrived at are therefore not beyond criticism, and too much importance should not be attached to an isolated date. But when several dates agree, the degree of probability is obviously greater. There are thus good reasons for thinking that the beginning of the Upper Palaeolithic in Europe may be placed between 35,000 and 40,000 years before our era. Previous estimates varied between 25 and 60,000. There is no doubt, then, that some progress has been made.

Potassium-argon method uses the potassium isotope $K^{40}$, which breaks down to form argon at a rate such that in 1,330,000,000 years half the atoms have been transformed. Here is a method capable of covering the greater part of geological time, and not simply the Quaternary Period; but it is only applicable to sediments that are rich in potassium, for example volcanic ash. This method

20

*Figure 3* Section at Combe-Grenal (Dordogne) showing the archaeological layers. The present shelter is in the background.

*Figure 4* Evolution
from the chopping-tool
to the handaxe
by development of
the bifacial retouch.

has been used to date the strata at Olduvai in East Africa, and the result was surprising: the age of the Australopithecan layers was double the expected figure – between 1·2 and 1·9 million years. But there are enough coherent measures to suggest that this is something like the right order of magnitude.

When applied to more recent levels, this method has sometimes produced absurd results in conflict with geological data and the dates given by radioactive carbon. For example, the Magosian, an industry belonging at most to the end of the Palaeolithic, was dated at 276,000 years which is absolutely impossible. It would seem that for figures below 400 to 500,000 years, the results obtained by this method can only be accepted with the greatest caution.

There is accordingly a large gap between the dates given by radioactive carbon and by potassium. Other methods (uranium – thorium – protactinium, for example) give dates going almost back to 700,000, but can only be applied at present to marine deposits, which it is always tricky to correlate with deposits on land.

Just as stratigraphy remains the basis of palaeolithic chronology, so typology must remain the basis of any study of industry. Typology is the science that makes it possible to define, recognise and classify the different varieties of implement encountered in prehistoric deposits. It is a difficult but indispensable discipline. It is quite certain that if one wishes to compare two industries, there must first be a quite positive knowledge of the types of instrument to be met with in each of them. There is no becoming a typologist in a hurry, any more than one can become a geologist or an ethnographer in a hurry. Many publications reporting excellent excavation-work have been made almost useless by a poor knowledge of typology. And as two objects that are morphologically identical may well have been fashioned according to different techniques, it is as well to be knowledgeable about the technical methods of stone-flaking. Experimental research work has been

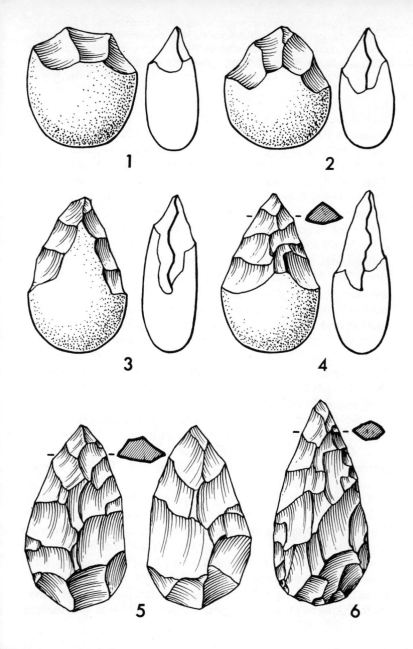

*Figure 5* 1, direct percussion flaking with a hammerstone. 2, pressure
flaking; the hand which holds the tool, protected by a piece of leather,
is held against the left knee, the right knee pushing the hand
which holds the retoucher. 3, direct percussion with a soft hammer
(wood, bone). The angle under which the flint is struck is very different.

carried out on this subject ever since the study of prehistory
began. In the last fifty years, one might mention Barnes, Noone
and H. Warren in England; Coutier, Bordes and Tixier in France;
Don Crabtree in America – among many others. Knowledge of
these techniques makes it possible to distinguish in a given object
the accidental from the intentional. Unfortunately, a great many
prehistorians have not understood the need for this distinction.

The first human tools were roughly worked pebbles, prepared by
chipping off some flakes on one or on both sides so as to obtain a
cutting edge (see figure 10). Because of the small size of these
stones, the work was no doubt done by simple percussion, using
another stone as the hammer (see figure 5, 1). Later on, the
worked part began to occupy a larger and larger part of the stone's
surface, and then the whole of it, thus producing in the first place
handaxes with an unworked butt, and then handaxes flaked over
their entire surface (see figure 4). At some unspecified time (for
this discovery must have been made on several occasions) towards
the end of the Lower Acheulean, man discovered a most important
fact, namely that stone (and flint in particular) can be more
effectively chipped by using as a hammer something less hard than
itself, such as bone, horn, deer-antlers, or hard wood, so making it
possible to work on the cutting face at a more acute angle and
obtain a flatter finished product (see figure 5, 3). This was how the
Solutreans chipped the greater part of their laurel-leaves.

At a late date no doubt – for there is no absolute proof of this
before the Solutrean – man discovered how to finish off a surface
by using pressure. Instead of striking the object, one presses on its
edge with a bone or ivory tool, or even with a piece of hard wood
(see figure 5, 2). This technique can only be applied to fairly small
objects, for under normal conditions it is difficult to obtain flakes
more than 5 cm long and 1·5 cm wide. But this is a much better way
than striking to produce a regular surface. There is an intermediate

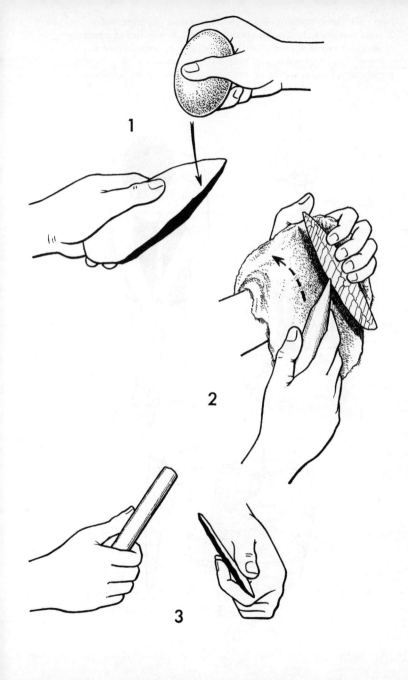

1

2

3

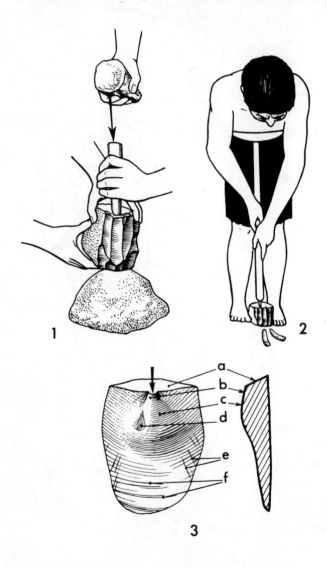

*Figure 6* 1, indirect percussion (punch technique) for obtaining blades. 2, chest-pressure technique for obtaining blades. 3, principal characteristics of the lower face of a flake: *a*, striking platform; *b*, percussion cone; *c*, conchoid (bulb) of percussion; *d*, splinter; *e*, striations; *f*, ondulations, the concavity of which is always toward the percussion cone.

technique known as indirect percussion, when a bone or wooden chisel is placed between the striker and the object to be trimmed (see figure 6, 1). The study of the waste flakes often allows us to know the technique or techniques which were used.

Apart from bifacially flaked artefacts, palaeolithic industries include a large quantity of implements made from flakes or blades. These flakes may be obtained in various ways. One may either strike the stone with a hand-hammer made of stone, wood or bone; or one may use a fixed object, such as a large stone on the ground, against which the flint nodule is struck. (This is also known as the anvil technique.) The flint from which flakes are struck is called the core. The flake reveals characteristic features on the lower surface (see figure 6, 3). The striking-platform of the core is defined as the surface which is struck in order to detach a flake. It may be fixed, or variable, if the surface exposed by removing the previous flake is then used in its turn as the new striking platform.

A flake more than twice as long as it is wide is called a blade. These are more common in the Upper Palaeolithic, but they appear sporadically very early on, in the Middle Acheulean, and even in the Lower. Of course there may always be the chance of accidental blades from the earliest period onwards.

There are several types of core, more or less characteristic of the large divisions of the Palaeolithic period. They start by being shapeless or globular, then become discoid or Levallois, then pyramidal or prismatic (see figure 8), these latter types reaching their true development in the Upper Palaeolithic. The Levallois technique has often been imperfectly understood, and requires a few words of explanation. It does not consist, as has often been thought, in preparing the striking-platform by chipping off small facets, but in pre-determining the form of the flake by a careful preparation of the upper surface of the core (figure 8, 3,4). The striking-platform, hence the butt of the flake, is often faceted, but it

*Figure 7* Cumulative graph of a Quina-type Mousterian (blue line) and a denticulate Mousterian (red line). The numbers at the bottom refer to a typological list of sixty-two types of flake tools. It can be seen at once that the Quina Mousterian is very rich in side-scrapers (numbers 9 to 29) and the denticulate Mousterian is rich in notches (number 42) and denticulated tools (number 43) and poor in scrapers.

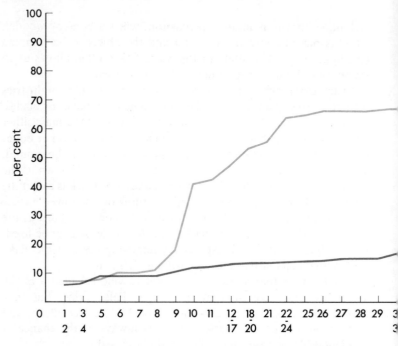

may perfectly well be smooth; yet the flake is none the less Levallois in type. Flakes have been obtained by direct striking. Good blades may be obtained by this technique, but more regular ones may be had by indirect striking (see figure 6, 1). In the case of obsidian, or in order to produce small flint blades, chest pressure may be used (see figure 6, 2). These flakes or blades may have been used just as they were, but they were more often transformed into specialised tools by retouching. This retouching as in the case of bifacial tools could be done by direct percussion (various striking-instruments being used), or by working against a fixed 'anvil', or by pressure.

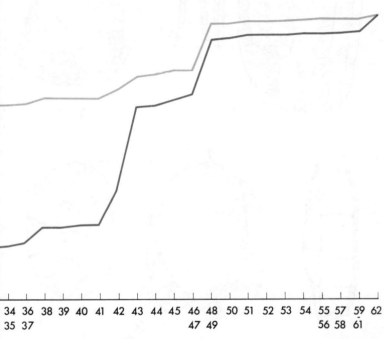

34 36 38 39 40 41 42 43 44 45 46 48 50 51 52 53 54 55 57 59 62
35 37                          47 49                    56 58 61

The classic archaeological method, based upon qualitative criteria, was used for a long time for the study of industries. The most striking finds were described at length, and compared with one another from site to site, and 'characteristic types' were thus laid down for each industry. Although the best writers such as Peyrony, Breuil and Commont often tried to look at the material they were studying as a whole, quantitative data were rarely taken into account. Certain prehistorians, such as J. Bouyssonie, made a point of giving percentages for the various implements, but they hardly made any use of them for comparisons. Others gave percentages, but arbitrarily included among them implements,

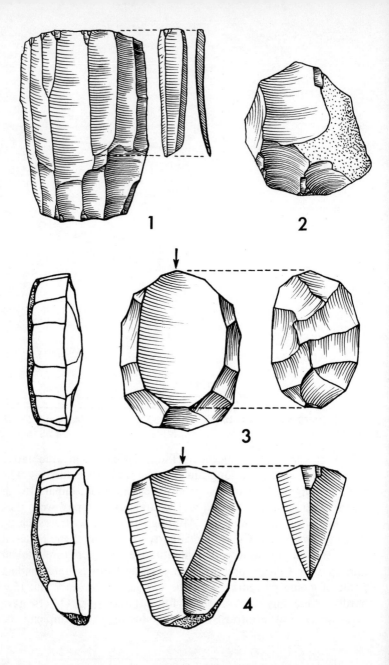

1

2

3

4

*Figure 8* 1, prismatic blade core (Upper Palaeolithic); 2, globular core; 3, Levallois flake core, with the flake beside it; 4, special Levallois core for the production of Levallois points. (3 and 4: Mousterian.)

un-retouched flakes, cores, striking-instruments etc. . . . . a procedure which robbed them of much of their significance. Quantitative studies on the different techniques were made by Barnes and Kidder as early as 1936, but were not followed up.

The study of prehistory soon showed as it developed the dangers of correlations based only upon 'characteristic implements'. Moreover, this method did not make it possible to follow the evolution of a particular industry. For instance, as soon as some Gravette points were found in a Perigordian level, this level was classified as Perigordian IV. In 1948–50 we introduced the systematic use of statistical methods into palaeolithic study. Similar researches have since been undertaken by various authors in different countries (figure 7 gives an example of a graphical representation used by the Bordeaux group). These simple statistical methods make it possible to concentrate on a single sheet of paper or in a graph the chief technical and typological characteristics of an industry. At the moment more advanced research using statistical methods is going forward in France, England and the United States.

The results coming from the introduction of quantitative methods presuppose – even more than did the classical methods – an elaborate and faultless typology. And so typological research, which seemed to have had its day, has once more come into favour.

# 3 Africa – the cradle of mankind ?

At the present time, Africa would seem to have been the cradle of the human race; but, as Abbé Breuil liked to observe, this cradle is a cradle on wheels. New research in the Pliocene and Villafranchian layers among the Siwalik Hills in the north of the Indian Peninsula may well lead one day to the discovery of a new ancestral form of humanity belonging to lower strata than those in Africa, which date from the Upper Villafranchian.

The story begins in 1924 with the chance discovery by a quarryman, M. de Bruyn, of a small skull which was sent to Raymond Dart, Professor of Anatomy at Johannesburg University. This skull came from Taungs, to the north of Kimberley (see figure 9, 18). It was incomplete, but the face was well preserved and there was a natural endocranial cast. In spite of the very primitive characteristics of these remains, Dart thought that he recognised certain human features, particularly in the teeth, and concluded this must be an intermediate form between the higher apes and man. But Dart hardly found any support, except from Broom, a South African palaeontologist, and the general opinion remained that this *Australopithecus Africanus* was a strange anthropoid.

In 1936 Broom announced that he had discovered in breccia filling up an ancient cave at Sterkfontein, west of Johannesburg, part of a skull reminiscent of the one found at Taungs, but this time of an adult, which he first named *Australopithecus*, and subsequently *Plesianthropus transvaalensis*. One discovery followed another, and at Kromdraai, near Sterkfontein, there was discovered a different and distinctly larger type, *Paranthropus robustus* and in 1947, at Swartkrans in the same region, a still larger form, *Paranthropus crassidens*. In 1947 Dart also discovered in the breccia of the Limeworks cave at Makapansgat, 200 kilometres north of Pretoria, various portions belonging to a type he named *Australopithecus prometheus*, for he thought (wrongly, as it proved) that it was associated with traces of fire. Finally in 1952 there was again found at Swartkrans, at the same level as the australopithecines, a mandible which Broom and Robinson considered definitely human and belonging to another type, *Telanthropus capensis*. There have been other finds since then, and the australopithecines are amongst the most numerous and best known of man's possible ancestors. Apart from *Telanthropus*, nowadays identified with *Pithecanthropus*, two forms are generally recognised as genera or sub-genera, *Australopithecus* (which now embraces *Plesianthropus*), and *Paranthropus*. Taungs, Sterkfontein and Makapansgat are often placed in the Villafranchian, whilst Swartkrans and Kromdraai would be a little more recent, and date from the beginning of the Middle Pleistocene. The fauna found along with *Australopithecus* varies from site to site, and generally comprises other primates (especially baboons), rodents, insectivores, hyracoids; numerous carnivores (including hyenas and sabre-toothed felines), suidae, the *Sivatherium* (a kind of short-necked giraffe), sometimes equidae, and sometimes numerous antilopes.

The cranial capacity of the australopithecines varies from 435 to 600 cubic centimetres, and averages 500. It is to be noted that *Paranthropus*, one and a half times as large as *Australopithecus*, has no higher index capacity. The largest cranial capacity known among the anthropomorphs is to be found among the gorilla's – 710 cc; and although the gorillas are giants, their average is only 500 cc. With *Pithecanthropus*, it varies from 775 to 1,200. So, from this point of view the australopithecines come in between. Their head combines a brain-case which is still not very capacious, a prognathous face, and powerful mandibles, which gives them an ape-like appearance. But a series of characteristics bring them close to man. *Australopithecus* has no pronounced supra-orbital torus, nor a sagittal crest, while these characteristics exist in *Paranthropus*. The Foramen magnum is placed well forward, which is not so in the anthropoids; this would point to an upright posture. The dentition is primitive but human. The real surprise comes in the bones of the pelvis and lower limbs, which also point to an upright posture. One would have expected that with such a primitive cranium, the australopithecines would have walked in a stooping position like the anthropomorphs, for according to the classic theory, the brain should have developed before perfect upright posture could be attained. But this did not prove to be so: these beings with very primitive brains walked upright, thus freeing their hands and enabling them to run in a way not possible for the large apes. Their manner of life must accordingly have been very different from that of the gorillas or chimpanzees.

Unlike the anthropoid apes, who were forest-dwellers, the australopithecines in South Africa must have lived in a relatively dry and almost desert-like region, especially in their earlier forms; whilst a study of the sediments in the case of the Kromdraai forms shows that the climate was moister, corresponding perhaps to a pluvial period.

Judging from the particular features of the teeth, it has been generally thought that *Paranthropus* was a vegetarian, whilst *Australopithecus* added to his diet small animals and the young of larger species. There is nothing impossible about this, for baboons are occasionally carnivorous. The comparative frequency of various bones in the Australopithecine caves would seem to indicate that they are – partly at any rate – the remains of meals. Not only did he hunt small animals, but – with free hands and able to run at a comparatively rapid pace – he was no doubt capable of seizing the remains of meals left behind by the larger wild animals. The first men were probably scavengers. Amongst the remains of baboons, there are a fair number of skulls showing fractures and dents such as might have been caused by a blow from a club, but do not appear to be the result of natural causes. Dart thinks the australopithecines used animal teeth, horns and bones as weapons and

*Figure 9* Position of some African sites: 1, Sidi Abderrhamane;
2, Ternifine; 3, Sidi Zin; 4, Tabelbala, Techenghit;
5, Erg Tihodaine; 6, Hagfet ed Dabba; 7, Haua Fteah; 8, Kharga;
9, Wanyanga; 10, Omo; 11, Olorgesailie; 12, Olduvai; 13, Isimila;
14, Kalambo Falls; 15, Broken Hill; 16, Makapansgat;
17, Sterkfontein; 18, Taungs; 19, Fauresmith; 20, Stillbay.

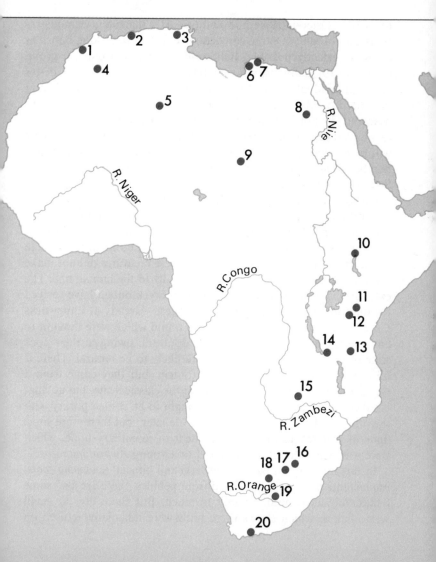

tools (the Osteodontokeratic culture). His ingenious demonstrations do not always carry conviction, but the use of long bones as clubs is perfectly possible. Baboon-hunting would imply a group existence, for baboons, who would be much stronger and better armed individually than the australopithecines themselves, live in organised bands. The bones found in caves are often split lengthwise and do not bear the marks of any carnivorous teeth; could this have been done to extract the marrow? A great many points will be cleared up when proper excavations have been made at a number of sites, for at present the majority of the finds (except at Sterkfontein and Swartkrans) were made in the course of industrial operations in the limestone from which the caves are hollowed out.

Until recently, no stone implements had been found in the australopithecine caves in South Africa. And so – with the reservation that long bones may have been used as clubs and natural stones to break the bones – it was thought that these creatures did not make tools, although they belonged anatomically to the human line. The excavations by Robinson and Mason at Sterkfontein have revived the question and not set the matter at rest. Already at Limeworks Cave some dolomite-stones had been found which were thought to have been chipped; but this is very doubtful, owing to their poor state of preservation – they are more likely to be natural. There is no doubt about the tools at Sterkfontein, but they come from a reddish-brown breccia which is not at the classical site, but at what is called 'the extension', and was thought to be contemporary with the principal layer. In reality, it is a little later; but there were some finds of isolated teeth and a fragment of maxilliary bone, which were somewhat doubtfully referred to a young *Australopithecus*.

In this industry unifacial (*choppers*) and bifacial (*chopping-tools*) implements have been fashioned from pebbles, there are also some flakes that have been roughly trimmed. But there are no small waste flakes, which shows these tools were not manufactured on the spot. There are also rock pebbles not normally found on the site: twenty-four of them were unworked and twenty-three fractured in course of use. Some of the tools show battered edges. Are these a sign of hard usage, for example in breaking bones, or of clumsiness when they were being chipped into shape? Desmond Clark leans towards the latter explanation; and it is certain that beginners in the art of stone-chipping often do get battered edges. The tools seem to be concentrated in the western part of the site, near the ancient entrance to the cave. The fact that these stone choppers are sharpened on both faces makes them comparable with the Oldowan finds (see below), but more elongated specimens made Mason wonder whether they might not belong to a very ancient level of the handaxe cultures. This would fit in very well with the date indicated by the fauna, which belongs to the Middle Pleistocene Period. But in that case, were they made by the australopithecines, or by more advanced forms like *Telanthropus*? As we shall presently see, the discoveries in East Africa indicate that certain of the australopithecines at least possessed tools. In any case the fauna remains at these sites show not only that the australopithecines were scavengers, but also that they hunted the smaller species. Such carnivorous habits would require sharp instruments for cutting through the skin and getting at the flesh, for the australopithecines had no strong canine or incisor teeth (see figure 10, 3).

Did they really live in caves, or did they merely visit them in search of water in this arid countryside, as Clark has suggested? The fact that the remnants of animal bones only contain certain parts of the animal would point to this being a habitat to which only certain select portions were brought in. K. P. Oakley has pointed out that in the absence of fire – of which there are no traces – a cave is a perfect trapping-place for small primates, and that they would have been easy prey for the carnivores. It may be that if they really hunted the baboon, they must, like them, have lived in bands, and that concerted stone-throwing concentrated on the narrow entrance to the cave would have driven off any large wild animals.

Even before the australopithecine discoveries it was thought that there had been found in Africa a very ancient stone industry, showing flaking on one side only, particularly in the ancient alluvial deposits of the Kafu River, in Uganda (E. J. Wayland, 1919). Since then abundant traces have been found in a number of places – too abundant in fact – and it would now appear that these Kafuan stones were largely produced by natural causes. Others, which are more clearly defined, undoubtedly belong to the Oldowan.

This is how matters now stand for South Africa; but since 1959 the centre of interest as far as prehumans are concerned has shifted to East Africa. In Tanzania (formerly Tanganyika), 36 km NNE of Lake Eyasi, near the eastern branch of the Rift Valley, there is a deep gorge cutting into the Serengeti plain and through the sediments of the Lower Pleistocene. This is the Olduvai (or Oldoway) gorge, representing the finest sequence in the world of material from the Lower Palaeolithic period. It is forty kilometres long, and from 100 to 130 metres deep, and was discovered in 1911 by the German Kattwinkel (who found fossil bones there) subsequently being partially explored by Professor Hans Reck in 1913. Research work was resumed after the war by Louis Leakey. Born in 1903, the son of a missionary, Leakey was brought up among the Kikuyu, then studied at Cambridge and produced a thesis on the Stone Age in Kenya. He returned to Africa in 1924 and distinguished himself by various discoveries, particularly by the famous human remains found at Kanam and Kanjera, though their age and attribution to *Homo sapiens* were not accepted by a number of anthropologists. A man of energy and enthusiasm, he organised a first expedition to Olduvai in 1931 together with Reck, and in the same year discovered traces of the Oldowan industry (see figure 10).

*Figure 10* 1, chopping-tool from Olduvai, layer i; 2, chopping-tool evolving into a handaxe, Olduvai, layer ii; 3, tool from Sterkfontein; 4, chopper from the Vallonet cave.

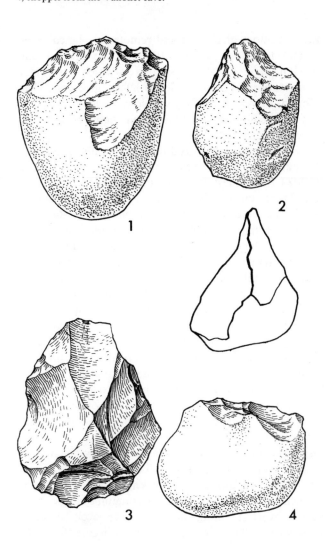

In spite of the difficulties of climate and remoteness, he collected numerous animal fossils of the greatest possible interest and established a whole series of palaeolithic levels which have made Olduvai a central point for palaeolithic study in Africa. But although he found many traces of human activity, he did not find the remains of the beings who had fashioned these tools. Yet in the end patience is always rewarded.

On 17 July 1959, when Leakey was unwell and confined to camp, Mrs Mary Leakey went to the excavation site known as FLK I, which had yielded the earliest traces of the Oldowan during the 1931–2 season. There, on a slope, she noticed the fragment of a temporal bone in the scree, and higher up three teeth *in situ* in the layer. Leakey, forgetting all about his indisposition, hastened to the scene of the discovery, and up to 22 August he and his wife continued to find fragments enough to allow the reconstruction of an almost complete skull, with only the mandible missing. And – what was particularly important – this skull was found on a living floor; and in the part so far excavated they found nine Oldowan implements, 176 flakes and a hammerstone. There were also un-worked stones of rocks not belonging to the site, and the bones of small animals or the young of larger species. And almost all these bones were broken or cleft along their length (figure 11).

The skull belonged to an individual about sixteen years old, whom Leakey christened *Zinjanthropus Boisei* (Zinj being an ancient Arab name for East Africa, and Charles Boise the partial financer of the excavation).

This deposit was found about 6·50 metres below the top of layer I at this spot, and this layer, which, like layer II, was formerly ascribed to the Middle Pleistocene, is now known to belong to the Upper Villafranchian, and may therefore be contemporary with the australopithecine levels at Taungs and the lower levels of Sterk-fontein and elsewhere. Here, then, an australopithecine (for Zing, as he is called for short, is very close to *Paranthropus*,) was beyond any doubt directly associated with a stone-working industry.

It will be as well to say a few words on the Olduvai stratigraphy before examining the later discoveries. The layers rest upon basalt lava that came from the neighbouring volcanoes. Beginning at the lowest and working upwards, we have:

Bed I:    This is sometimes about 40 metres thick, and composed of volcanic tuff separated into two parts by a layer of redeposited tuff. This layer yielded four Oldowan levels.

Bed II:   This covers Bed I conformably, and the two are some-times difficult to separate. It varies in composition, being at times entirely lacustrine and sterile, at times composed of redeposited tuffs or various fluviatile (water laid) or aeolian (wind deposited) sediments. The lower part is separated from the middle and upper by an aeolian level. It varies in thickness from place to place between 20 and 30 metres, and contains several archaeological levels – Oldowan at its base, 'Chelleo-acheulean' in the higher levels. There is a slight disconformity at the top.

Bed III:  This is 10 to 15 metres thick, and is composed of chiefly fluviatile sediments, with some aeolian admixture. There are infrequent traces of 'Chelleo-acheulean' industry.

Bed IV:   This is about forty-five metres thick, it is fluviatile at the base and aeolian at the top, the record of a semi-desert environment. It contains various Acheulean levels.

Then there is evidence of various tectonic movements which were already beginning towards the top of Bed II, producing faults and a general disconformity. Bed V, thought to belong to the Gamblian (last pluvial) and to the later pluvial phases, contains some 'Kenya Capsian' and is definitely more recent. It consists principally of aeolian sand. Some authorities also distinguish a Bed VI. The Olduvai fauna in Bed I and the lower part of Bed II is Upper

Villafranchian; but certain archaic forms persist up to the end of Bed IV.

From the point of view of chronology, the Olduvai Gorge held a great surprise. The age of the South African australopithecines had been estimated at between 700 and 900,000 years. But the measurements carried out at Olduvai by the potassium-argon method gave results of a completely different order of magnitude; for the base of Bed I gave a date of about 1,900,000 years, and *Zinjanthropus* would be about 1,750,000 years old. The base of Bed II would probably be earlier than 1,110,000 years. All these dates are about twice as high as expected, but although this method can only be applied with some caution for dates less than 400 or 500,000 years the different measurements obtained for the Villafranchian at Olduvai and elsewhere would seem to tally satisfactorily.

Thanks to the Leakeys' dogged researches, there are now a whole series of human remains that have been discovered at Olduvai. Bed I has yielded two different types of hominid. From the bottom upwards, there were finds of teeth belonging to *Australopithecus* (*Homo habilis*); then about the middle of the layer a form called by Leakey first of all *Pre-Zinjanthropus* (because it was found at a lower level than Zinj), and then *Homo habilis*. The majority of anthropologists agree in bringing it within the genus *Australopithecus*. In this Bed I there are also remains of *Zinjanthropus* ( = *Paranthropus*). In Bed II, from the bottom upwards Leakey's *Homo habilis* is present, but F. Clark Howell, Robinson, Tobias and Von Koenigswald think this may be an ancient form of a small stature *Pithecanthropus* (*Homo Erectus*). Higher up in Bed II, another *Homo habilis* is likewise a *Pithecanthropus*. In the second part of Bed II there is a large and undoubted *Pithecanthropus* skull. It would seem that we are watching the evolution of *Australopithecus* into *Pithecanthropus* by way of increasing stature and

*Figure 11* The *Zinjanthropus* floor at Olduvai, bed I. Antelope horn bones, bones and flakes (Excavations by M. and L. Leakey).

cranial capacity. Leakey and Tobias are however of the opinion that from the base of Bed I upwards, the form named *Homo habilis* was already more evolved than the australopithecines of South Africa, and already definitely human, as the chosen name implies. It is also important to note that *Paranthropus* continues to the top of Bed II, and is therefore contemporary with the Pithecanthropines. In the lower part of Bed IV, but fairly high up in it, are the remains of a more evolved type, more or less reminiscent of the European Neanderthal man or the African Broken Hill man, with Acheulean tools (figure 12).

If *Pithecanthropus* seems certainly to have been responsible for the handaxe industries that appeared during his time (at the base of Bed II it is still Oldowan; see figure 10, 2), we are left wondering whether it was *Australopithecus* or *Paranthropus* who flaked the tools in Bed I, or whether both had a hand in it. It is probable that the former stands in line of human descent proper, whilst the second – who was more primitive – was an evolutionary dead-end. There are strong probabilities that only *Australopithecus* was the author of the tools, and it may well be that the skull of *Paranthropus* (*Zinjanthropus*) found on the site at FLK I in the middle of the implements is not that of their maker, but of the victim, among the instruments that were used to cut him in pieces. But the question has not been finally settled; and there may perhaps have been two tool-makers on the earth at a certain moment of time in the Lower Pleistocene period.

Bed I contains no handaxes even of the crudest sort, as far as our present knowledge goes, but pieces similar to those found at a number of other sites. This Oldowan industry continues on into the lower parts of Bed II. It is more particularly based upon the shaping of round stones, hence the term 'pebble culture', which was applied equally to the Oldowan and the Kafuan at a time when the latter was thought to be an ancestor of the Oldowan. But there are also implements shaped from chert nodules, quartz and quartzite, etc.

Of course there are also flakes, if only from the chipping of the stones, and sometimes these flakes have been put to use and show the marks of it. Some of the Bed I flakes have even been turned into rough scrapers and other kinds of implement. Among the pebble tools, some have been worked on one side only, from flat stones, and others on both sides (figure 10, 1, 2).

Apart from the tools proper, showing marks of use, there are natural stones coming from other places, probably partly intended for the same purposes, and some bone fragments which were also probably put to use. One of them shows traces of rubbing and has acquired a certain polish.

In site DK I, in the lower part of Bed I, a rough circle of loosely-piled stones was discovered. It is possible that this was a rough basis for a wind screen, the stones having been placed at the bottom to keep it in place.

According to Clark, the simple nature of the industries in Bed I shows that there is no need to postulate a long period of experimentation and more rudimentary tools before the appearance of the Oldowan. Oakley also thinks that this industry represents the oldest attempts at tool-making. Theoretically, however, one could imagine an even more elementary stage, when – after using natural stones, as the apes do – their users began to select naturally broken stones with a sharp edge, before the idea emerged that a sharp edge could be *obtained at will* by striking the edge of a stone. This discovery may well have been a chance one, when some natural stone broke as it was being used to smash a bone. And this experience may have been repeated many times before some australopithecine genius reproduced the effect deliberately. It is possible that not all the australopithecines had tools, since as we have seen there is some doubt about those in South Africa. It would be difficult to adduce proof of this stage of the use of naturally-formed tools, if it did really exist; for there is not much difference between a stone with a natural chip and one from which a flake has been removed by man.

Thus in the East African Upper Villafranchian, the most primitive tools so far discovered occur at the same time as the prehuman forms. There is thus a certain inclination at present to think that the human adventure began somewhere among the savannahs of Africa, whence this basic discovery – the purposely fashioned implement – spread rapidly across the tropical zones of the Old World.

In Africa important discoveries have also been made outside the specially-favoured districts we have just been examining. In March

| | Beds | Hominid remains | Living sites | Industries | K/A dates |
|---|---|---|---|---|---|
| | | | | | (millions of years) |
| UPPER PLEISTOCENE | Bed IV | Homo* cf. Broken Hill (?) | VEK* | | |
| MIDDLE PLEISTOCENE | Bed III | | | | |
| MIDDLE PLEISTOCENE | Upper Bed II | Paranthropus* | TK. BK II* FLK II SHK II | OLD TO UPPER ACHEULEAN | |
| | | | CK | | |
| | | | FLK S II | | |
| | | Homo erectus* | LLK II* | | 0·49 |
| | Aeolian | | | | |
| FINAL AND UPPER VILLAFRANCHIAN | Lower Bed II | Homo erectus.* Paranthropus* | MNK II** | OLDOWAN | 1·1 |
| | | | FLK II.N1 | | |
| | | Homo (Pithecanthropus) erectus?* | FLK-Maiko Gully* | | |
| | | | FLK-N1 | | |
| | Bed I | Paranthropus (Zinjanthropus)* + Australopithecus* | FLK Main** | OLDOWAN | |
| | | Australopithecus (Pre-Zinjanthropus)* | FLK N.N.1* | | 1·75 |
| | | Australopithecus (Homo) habilis* | WK. DK·MK* | | 1·85 |
| | Basalt | | | | |

6 SURFACES

*Figure 12* Position of human remains and main living sites in Olduvai stratigraphy (following F. Clark Howell).

47

1961, M. Yves Coppens discovered in Chad, 600 kilometres north-east of Fort-Lamy, a cranium and facial bone fragments of a being similar both to the *Australopithecus* and to *Pithecanthropus*, which was provisionally christened *Tchadanthropus uxoris* ('the Tchad man of the wife', for it was in fact discovered by Madame Coppens). He would appear to come in on the evolutionary line between *Australopithecus* and *Pithecanthropus*, and – to judge by the associated fauna – might be dated about 1,000,000 years ago. He would thus be more or less contemporary with the human remains found at the base of Bed II at Olduvai. There were no signs of associated industry, but he would seem to have lived on the fringes of the vast lacustrine basin of which Lake Chad is only a remnant; and in the same region implements of the Oldowan type have been found.

Africa abounds in deposits yielding traces of this primitive industry, but no human remains. In East Africa, apart from Olduvai and the neighbouring sites, there are the Omo layers in Southern Ethiopia, near Lake Rudolf (Clark Howell). This industry also crops up in the Sahara, often in surface sites, though rather less certainly. In 1947 Professor Arambourg found at Ain-Anech in Algeria, alongside a Villafranchian fauna, a quantity of spheroid stones on average as big as an orange. The same site has also produced some very rough handaxes from an unknown but probably later level. A pebble tool industry, with spheroids and flakes, was discovered by G. Laplace in the probably Villafranchian travertines of the Mansourah plateau, near Constantine. The travertine is covered by a gravel which contains some massive handaxes as well as spheroids. At Casablanca in Morocco spheroid stones have been found, with classical pebble implements of the Oldowan type. Here, as at Olduvai, we seem to be able to follow the evolution toward the handaxes in the later levels. In South Africa, the ancient alluvial deposits of the Vaal River have also yielded pebble implements.

There have also been finds in the Middle East. At Ubeidiya in the Jordan valley, on the right bank about thirty kilometres south of Tiberias, there have been discovered, with Villafranchian or perhaps slightly later fauna, pebble implements of both the unifacial and the bifacial type, trihedral flint handaxes, and some flake-tools. But there is no certainty about the chronology, and the presence of the handaxes would seem to place this industry with the Olduvai Bed II rather than with Bed I.

In Asia the pebble tool industries without handaxes persist over a long period, and at present none of these seems to be as old as in Africa. But bone remains have been found in Java (*Meganthropus*) and in China (teeth) which have sometimes been attributed to *Australopithecus*.

But there is a more important site, important because it is more certain in date and altogether outside Africa or Asia, in Provence (France), discovered by René Pascal on 18 April 1958, and studied by H. de Lumley, S. Gagnière, L. Barral and Pascal, though unfortunately it is poor in industry and altogether devoid of human remains. This is the Vallonet cave at Roquebrune-Cap-Martin, on the Mediterranean coast. On top of the pre-Villafranchian marine levels are some cave sediments formed under cold climatic conditions, with a fauna typical of the Upper Villafranchian, that is to say contemporary with Bed I and the bottom of Bed II at Olduvai. Along with this fauna were found scanty remains of industry, valuable in that they bear explicit witness to man in Europe at this very remote period. There are four flakes and five pebble-tools (see figure 10, 4). The authors also describe some tools made of purposely broken bones, and even talk of their being 'sawn'; but this hardly carries conviction.

We can also note as a possibility a flake found by R. Agache and Fr. Bourdier in 1959 in an old terrace on the Somme, along with a horse-tooth (*E. Stenonis*) which might therefore be of Villafranchian date, but could also be later, for this form of horse had a long life. There are perhaps also some traces of Villafranchian industry in Rumania. There is also an intriguing possibility in Italy, where at Monte-Peglia, very close to a Villafranchian outcrop, have been found two flakes and a chopper (A.C. Blanc).

The Vallonet deposits would certainly appear to be contemporary with the lower Olduvai layers, but the exact correlation between them presents a difficult problem. The palaeontological dating systems at present at our disposal are too rough to determine whether, within the Upper Villafranchian, which appears to have lasted a million years, the Vallonet finds are exactly contemporary with a particular level in Olduvai Bed I, or with the bottom of Bed II, or whether they are earlier or later. The sediments from this cave do not lend themselves to potassium-argon dating. This site at least proves that man (probably at the *Australopithecus* level) had spread, as early as the Upper Villafranchian period, over the whole of Africa, probably over southern Asia, and at any rate over the south of Europe. We are then faced with another problem: did this expansion take place before the tool discovery stage, or later? A number of anthropologists are reluctant to admit that this invention could have taken place independently at various places and times, and therefore think the expansion was later. We shall see, however, that certain inventions must have been made several times. If this expansion did occur later, then in what direction? It would seem more probably to have been from Africa to Asia and from Africa to Europe, since there are numerous *Australopithecus* remains in eastern or southern Africa, scanty and doubtful ones in Asia, and none in Europe or even in North Africa. But these beings were present there, for the tools prove it; and they are even plentiful in the Maghreb. The discovery of bone remains is to a large extent due to the chance factors affecting their preservation; and South Africa with its ancient caves and East Africa with lake shores sealed by volcanic ash are without doubt the most favourable territories for the preservation of fossils. The very ancient infillings in European caves are often no more than remnants that have escaped the numerous scourings resulting from the violent climatic changes of the Pleistocene period. It is also partly a matter of chance. Leakey searched for twenty-five years before finding anything. It is therefore possible that future discoveries will shift the centre of gravity of the human line towards the North or the East. One might say that in the race to find the cradle of humanity, Africa looks like being the favourite; but Asia and even Europe are outsiders of whom more will perhaps be heard.

# 4 The Abbevillian and Acheulean developments in Europe

According to our present knowledge, it would seem that the Old-owan stage was followed by the first branching out of the palaeo-lithic industries, one branch continuing the pebble-tool tradition, the other developing the handaxe tradition, following along the Abbevillian-Acheulean lines.

When the Olduvai industries have been published (which should no doubt be in the near future) the upper part of Bed II will furnish us with valuable documentation on the transition of the *chopping-tool* to the true handaxe (see figure 13). In his 1951 publication, Leakey distinguished at Olduvai eleven phases in the evolution of the handaxe industries; but it seems that recent excavations have thrown new doubts on a certain number of these stages. However, basing our conclusions on this first study and on Biberson's work at Casablanca, the transition would appear to have taken place as follows: first, a development of retouching all round the pebble, except at the butt, giving proto-handaxes; then the extension of this retouching to the whole upper and lower surface of the pebble; and finally a total retouching doing away with the butt altogether. Incidentally, this last feature is by no means constant, and right into the Mousterian period some handaxes keep their unchipped butt (figure 36, 11). For a long time the handaxe remains asym-metrical, trihedral in section, with one face flatter than the other; then it becomes symmetrical in section. But those that are asym-metrical in section persist right up to the end.

For the ancient rough-hewn handaxes, the term used in Europe had been Pre-Chellean and Chellean, but this was then abandoned. However, the word 'Chellean' continued in use in Africa for these early stages until it was decided quite recently to drop it and to call the whole handaxe series 'Acheulean', the first levels constituting the Lower Acheulean. This was a mistake, for the term 'Lower Acheulean' had long possessed a different meaning in Europe. The distinction between the Abbevillian (former Pre-Chellean) and the

*Figure 13*
Abbevillian handaxes
from Olduvai;
1, primitive type;
2, more evolved type.

Acheulean is often given as the appearance of flaking with a soft hammer. This dividing line is as good as any other – in fact, it is the only possible one; but we must be able to distinguish between soft-hammer and stone-hammer flaking, though this is not always easy.

It is at the Abbevillian stage that the handaxe industries are known in Europe, where for a long time – before the discovery of the Vallonet – they were the most ancient forms to be recognised with certainty. The principal site is at Abbeville (hence the name Abbevillian). There, in the forty-five metre terrace of the Somme, there was a site, though it was unfortunately discovered too early on by gravel exploitation. In fact, the gravel-pit yielded signs of industry around the 1880s, at a time when only the most characteristic objects were collected, rough tools and flakes being then unrecognised. Reading from bottom to top, in simplified form, it produced:

1 On the chalk, red fluviatile gravels, with an ancient fauna. D'Ault du Mesnil has recognised among them some 'coups de poing', (handaxes), much-worn and rounded.

2 Sandy greenish Marls.

3 White Marl with an ancient fauna, containing amongst others *Elephas meridionalis*, an archaic *Elephas antiquus*, the Etruscan rhinoceros, Merck's rhinoceros, hippopotamus, the archaic *E. stenonis*, the sabre-toothed tiger, *Cervus Solhilacus*, the Somme Deer, the giant beaver (*Trogontherium*). D'Ault du Mèsnil found 'abundant' signs of industry in the lower part of this marl. At the top there were traces of an ancient peaty soil, and then after a period of erosion came traces of a more recent cycle.

The fauna, although ancient, is more evolved than Villafranchian, and probably belongs to an interstadial period of the Mindelian ice-age. The industry consists of fairly rough handaxes, chipped with a stone hammer, often leaving a butt and having wavy

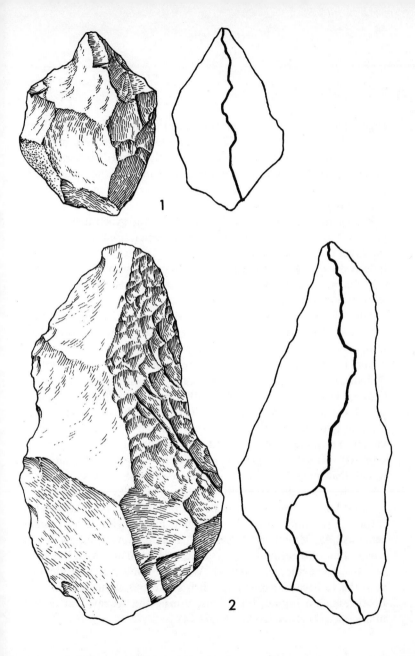

edges. These objects are often thick, and of uncertain morphology, for the form of the lump of flint has often had a strong influence upon it. Some of the handaxes are roughly pointed; others have a broad square end meant for cutting, and may be the ancestors of the bifacial Acheulean cleavers. These objects often carry broad cortex areas.

Basing himself on Coutier's stone-working experiments, Breuil put forth the idea (which, like all over-generalised ideas, became the rage) that these handaxes had been flaked against an anvil. It is indeed possible that this technique was used, but my own personal experiments have shown me that the same results can be produced with a hand-hammer.

The Abbevillian deposits must have contained flakes, but very few were at that time recovered. We do not know whether there were also stone tools of the Oldowan type; at this period, they would not in any case have been recognised. It is therefore very difficult to strike a parallel between Abbeville and any of the Olduvai layers. At present, Abbeville is the only known deposit *in situ*. Now and again bifacial implements of the Abbevillian type are found at various places, but they may be later than the Abbevillian. Yet there is no doubt at all that the Abbevillian does not represent an isolated group. In England in particular, sites are noted that may be Abbevillian, in a derived context. There is probably also some Abbevillian in the upper Garonne valley.

What human type was responsible for this industry? At Olduvai, it was a Pithecanthropus. But Abbeville has not yielded any human remains. At Mauer, in Germany, a human mandible was discovered in 1907, alongside a probably Mindelian fauna, but without any archaeological context. Without being precisely identical with the Pithecanthropus finds, it fits into this same general type. It represents a human type living during the Abbevillian period, about 500,000 years ago (see figure 14).

After the Abbevillian there is a gap in Europe, not due to an absence of population but to the scarcity of deposits during the interglacial periods. The implements left by man on the surface of the ground were carried away by the solifluctions of the next ice-age, and we come across them in derived positions in the river gravels.

We therefore know very little about the transition from the Abbevillian to the Acheulean, and about the Lower Acheulean stage. There are a few deposits dating from the end of the Mindel/Riss interglacial, which lasted a long time. In 1798 the famous Hoxne deposit in Suffolk had already yielded handaxes to John Frere. G. West's pollen researches have shown that the sands and lacustrine clays, where a number of the implements have been found, certainly belong to an interglacial period which can only be the Mindel/Riss. Other implements have been found in a solifluction level, and are considered by McBurney to be redeposited. But the freshness of some of them does not seem to confirm this opinion; and there are probably two levels, the second of them being Rissian. The implements were unfortunately described *en bloc*. There are some Lower Acheulean limandes (flat oval handaxes), and some delicate lanceolate handaxes which might be later, for like the cordiforms they recur in the Middle Acheulean.

Another deposit attributed to the end of the Mindel/Riss epoch is the one at Swanscombe, in the London suburbs. This attribution was partly made on account of the fauna, said to be temperate, and partly because of the now outmoded views of Breuil about the chronology of the Somme valley. There are certain facts in favour of this date, particularly the situation on a thirty-metre terrace near the present mouth of the Thames, which would point to a high water-level in the interglacial period; but other facts would seem to tell against it: in the first place, the advanced level of the industry. The position on a thirty-metre terrace might be due to an isostatic

56

*Figure 14* Human mandible found at Mauer (Germany) and belonging to a Pithecanthropus level in human evolution. Note the complete absence of any chin and the massivity of the bones.

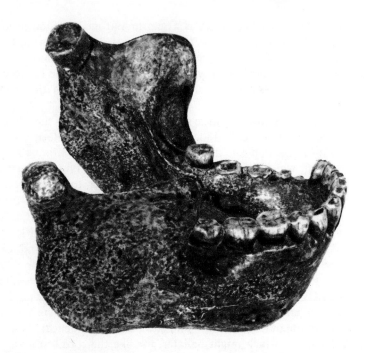

sinking of the British Isles under the weight of the Rissian glaciers, in which case the Swanscombe deposit might date from an inter-stadial stage of this ice-age. Certain writers would even place it in the Riss/Würm period. Along with an industry carrying a good number of handaxes of lanceolate or Micoquian style (see figure 16, 1), and flake-tools, there were found some very controversial human remains: the Swanscombe Man. Its stratigraphical position and its association with the Acheulean are certain, but its significance is much less so. What we have is a fragmentary skull in which the frontal part is lacking. The rounded and modern-looking shape of the occipital has raised the question whether the missing frontal

*Figure 15* Fragmentary Acheulean skull found at Swanscombe (England), seen from behind. This part of the skull is already very modern in shape, but we do not know the shape and aspect of the forehead.

bone was also modern in type. This rounded occipital is also found on the probably Rissian skull at Steinheim, in Germany, with a frontal bone of primitive type (figure 15).

Acheulean sites of the Rissian glaciation are very numerous, whether from the early part of the Riss in gravels, or later in the Older Loess. At Cagny, near Amiens, a level of solifluction dating from the very beginning of the Riss glaciation has yielded rich finds of industry *in situ*. The Acheuleans used to work the flint nodules found in the solifluction layer. The bifacial implements are often lanceolate or amygdaloid (almond-shaped) although there are some limandes (see figure 16, 5), and cordiforms. The flakes are for the most part produced in the making of bifacial implements, but there are also some which were deliberately flaked and often transformed into tools, such as scrapers, often well made, some end-scrapers, a few borers, atypical backed knives, and a good many notched tools or denticulates. But taken as a whole, the flake tools are somewhat rare. It should be noted that this is the first certain appearance of the Levallois technique for predetermining the form of the flake on the core. Not only are there proto-Levallois and Levallois flakes, but also some typical cores. The industry is like that at Swanscombe, or perhaps a little less advanced.

At a higher level, but still at the beginning of the Riss glaciation, must be placed the deposits at Saint-Acheul (the Amiens suburb that has given its name to the Acheulean), which produced the famous 'Commont's workshop' described by him from 1904 onwards. It is situated in the red sands beneath the Older Loess; and it is interesting to enumerate the objects recovered up to the end of December, 1905: 968 flakes, ninety-two cores, twenty hammers and seventy tools of various sorts, only fifteen of them being handaxes. It would seem that there is a turning-point in this Acheulean culture, when from this point onwards flake-tools become more numerous than the bifacial implements. Amongst the latter, there are some lanceolate handaxes of excellent quality, which would scarcely be surpassed in later ages. There are some scantier limandes, sometimes with twisted edges, numerous cordiforms, and a few bifacial cleavers. The flake-tools are quite varied: side-scrapers which are not very different from those found in the Mousterian, scrapers on the end of flakes, backed knives, 'becs', borers, burins and notched and denticulated implements (see figure 16, 2, 3, 4). But the Levallois technique seems absent, or very rare, although it exists at Cagny, which is an older deposit. This may be the level where there is a parting of the ways between the industries using the Levallois technique, and those where it is out of favour.

Also in the red sands, but in the Rue de Cagny, and a few hundred metres away, there is another deposit which differs in the proportion of handaxe types found, 271 out of 300 being limandes, often with twisted edges. Flake-tools are less plentiful. This is perhaps a different facies from the Middle Acheulean, or perhaps simply the reflection of different activities.

The Acheulean went on developing during the long Riss glaciation, which was interrupted by two marked temperate intervals. At the bottom of the third deposit of Older Loess, laid down in very cold conditions, there is in northern France an Upper Acheulean industry (see figure 16, 6) with fine handaxes, often lanceolate or Micoquian, in which the Levallois technique is fully developed.

The flake-tools – often on Levallois flakes – are numerous, and apart from the bifacial tools, it is almost impossible to distinguish this industry from certain Mousterian industries of the Würm glaciation.

In the valley of the Charente, in the south of France, there is an Acheulean industry not very different from that in the north. In the Garonne valley, quartzite pebbles are often used, giving it a rougher appearance. But there is also some Acheulean to be found in caves or shelters, in the Ardèche for example, at Orgnac (excavations by J. Combier), in the Hérault (at Aldène, where the deposit was destroyed by phosphate-working), at le Lazaret, at Nice, and at the Observatory cave at Monaco. In the Dordogne, the site at Combe-Grenal, in the valley of the Dordogne near Domme, has yielded fifty-five Mousterian layers, and nine Upper Acheulean layers of the Riss III period, with a rather peculiar facies. Although very rich in fine flake-tools, it is poor in bi-facial tools (five to eight per cent), most often amygdaloids, sometimes backed (figure 17, 1 to 6), recalling oriental forms. The La Chaise cave in the Charente has also yielded some Upper Acheulean of the Riss III period, fairly similar to that of Combe-Grenal. The Riss III fauna

*Figure 16 Middle Acheulean.* 1, handaxe from Swanscombe; 2, 3, 4, side-scraper, point and end-scraper of 'Commont's Workshop' at Saint-Acheul (Amiens, France); 5, 'limande' from Cagny (near Amiens). *Upper Acheulean.* 6, bifacial cleaver from Bihorel, near Rouen (France).

at Combe-Grenal, unlike that of Riss I and II, is a very cold-climate one, with abundant reindeer and some saiga antelope, but also some fallow-deer.

Interglacial deposits of the Riss/Würm are rarely preserved, for the same reasons as the Mindel/Riss deposits are rare. The tuffs of Celle-sous-Moret, south-east of Paris, have produced about twenty fine lanceolate handaxes which are dated by the flora. The interglacial sands and gravels of the Aisne, Oise and Somme valleys have yielded a whole series – sometimes in great abundance – of Upper Acheulean with finely flaked handaxes, flake-tools, Levallois flakes and blades and some backed blade-knives, which prefigure very early certain Upper Palaeolithic types (see figure 17, 7, 8).

The Acheulean extends into the beginning of the Würm glaciation, in the form of the Micoquian and Mousterian of Acheulean tradition, which we shall be considering later.

In Belgium there is some Middle and Upper Acheulean not very different from that of France and England. In Spain it is abundant; it shows such clear affinities with Africa that this can hardly be sheer coincidence. The Acheuleans very probably crossed the Straits of Gibraltar, which if it was not dry was at any rate narrower because of the low sea level during the glacial periods. The site at Torralba, about 100 kilometres north-east of Madrid, was discovered in 1907. This site and the neighbouring one at Ambrona were the object of recent excavation by Clark Howell. Both sites had been hunting-places, the Acheuleans having taken advantage of the marshy character for the hunting of the straight-tusked elephant. At Ambrona there were some fifty elephants that had been killed and cut up on the spot. The industry includes a good number of handaxes and cleavers on flakes of an African type, as well as flake tools. The excavators ascribe this deposit to the Upper Mindel glaciation, which is possible; but having visited it during the excavations, I do not see any overriding reasons for putting it

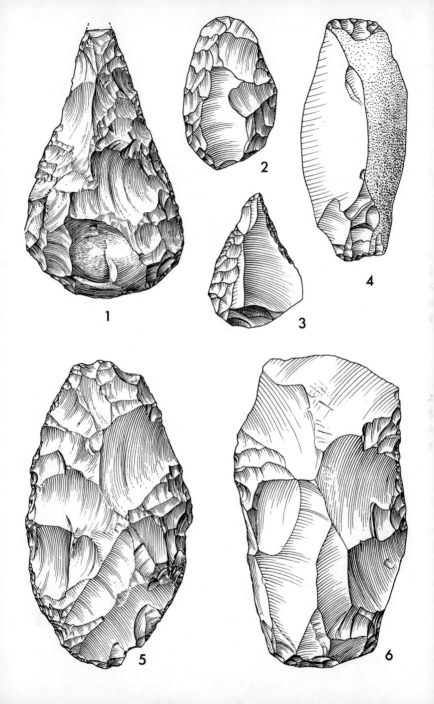

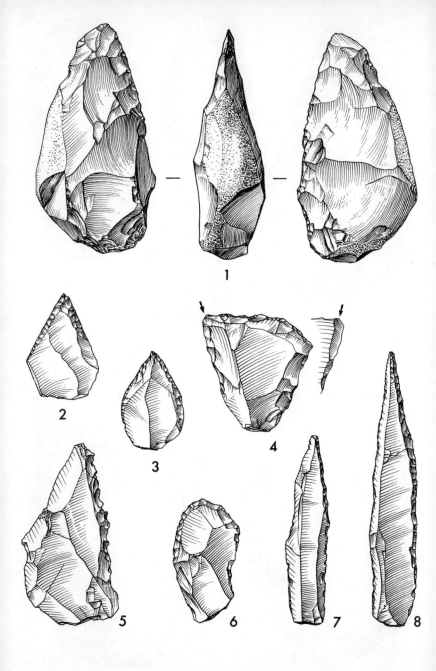

*Figure 17  Upper Acheulean.* 1, backed handaxe;
2,3, points; 4, burin; 5, denticulate tool;
6, end-scraper (all from the cave of
Combe-Grenal, Dordogne, France).
7,8, backed blades (from Moru, Oise, France).

further back than the Early Riss. Amongst other interesting details obtained by a very good excavation, it would seem that the Acheuleans used their victims' tusks as levers for moving the carcases and making it easier to cut them up (see figure 18). The Acheulean is also abundant in the valley of the Manzanares at Madrid.

There are several Acheulean deposits known in Italy, in particular the one at Venosa in the Basilicate (probably Upper Acheulean), and at Torre in Pietra near Rome, discovered and excavated by the great prehistorian and geologist Alberto Carlo Blanc, who unfortunately died before he was able to publish the details. There was an advanced 'Abbevillian' at the latter in solifluction levels, given as 430,000 years old by the potassium-argon method, and a Middle Acheulean industry with handaxes, chopping tools and scrapers, etc., probably Rissian. There was possibly a more ancient Acheulean industry at Capri. This Italian Acheulean has no African form.

As one approaches central and eastern Europe, the Acheulean becomes rarer. But there are still some important sites in Germany, particularly at Markkleeberg, near Leipzig. This is probably Rissian Acheulean, relatively poor in handaxes but rich in Levallois flakes. The rest of central Europe has only yielded a few traces, often rather late and not very convincing; and the same is true of eastern Europe. But at Cracovia-Wavel in Poland there is an Upper Acheulean or Micoquian industry dating from the last Interglacial, and a handaxe attributed to the Riss glaciation has been reported from Lower Silesia. Recently, some traces of Acheulean have been found in Greece. But as a whole, as far as Europe is concerned, the Acheulean would appear to be a western phenomenon.

# 5 The Acheulean in Africa

The Olduvai gorge has yielded a whole series of Acheulean levels; but for the same reason as was given for the older phases, we cannot examine them in detail, since the recent and yet unpublished excavations have brought important changes in the supposed sequence. They range between still primitive industries and a very advanced Acheulean stage, and almost from the start flake-cleavers play an important part.

East Africa has also provided a number of other spectacular sites, but most of them belong to an evolved or even late Acheulean period. At Isimila, in Tanzania, about 420 kilometres west of Dar-es-Salaam, there is a very fine site excavated by Clark Howell. The Acheuleans inhabited this spot at the edge of a small lake, at times drying out into marshland; there are various levels of habitat, but no traces of fire have been discovered. The larger tools (handaxes and cleavers) are often of very good quality, and the smaller ones (such as scrapers, discs, planes, spheroid stones, etc.) are found in percentages varying in different areas of the site. The handaxes and cleavers are often made from large flakes in which the butt is in an oblique position with respect to the axis of the whole, (see figure 20). There are often considerable variations in the proportions of the handaxes and cleavers, and we can but wonder whether these represent different traditions or different activities. Here too, as with the red sands at Saint-Acheul, the problem can be stated but not solved. It is clearly an Upper Acheulean stage, showing in its various levels some slight evolution towards a tendency for the ovate handaxes to decrease in number, and the elongated ovate and lanceolate handaxes to increase. There is only a very slight or even no evolution at all in the cleavers. This Acheulean industry already contains some tools reminiscent of the later Sangoan industry, particularly in various picks, planes, and chisels, though only in small percentages. This tendency towards the Sangoan type seems general throughout the whole of the Upper

Acheulean in central and eastern Africa (see figure 22).

One of the most spectacular sites is at Olorgesailie, in Kenya, sixty-four kilometres south-west of Nairobi, discovered by Mary Leakey. The Acheuleans occupied this site, also beside a lake. There are about a dozen levels, separated by sterile layers corresponding to the high-water levels of the lake. The industry as a whole corresponds to the Upper Acheulean. There are abundant handaxes and cleavers, and a variable percentage of smaller tools. Large spherical stones have been found in threes at various levels, which suggests their use as bolas-stones. On certain levels there are remains of industries comparable with those at Hope Fountain in Rhodesia, with some bifacial tools, six different kinds of scrapers, etc. Clark thinks that this represents a different activity, rather than a separate industry. Part of the habitat levels had been opened up by erosion and another part by the excavations, thus transforming the deposits into an open-air museum, with the objects left in place.

At Kariandusi, near Lake Nakuru, in the Rift Valley in Kenya, there is another equally well-protected Upper Acheulean deposit, with some obsidian tools. At the Lewa site, on the northern slopes of Mount Kenya, the tools are sometimes enormous. Acheulean material is found as far as Mombasa on the coast.

Another important site, situated in northern Rhodesia but on the borders of Tanzania, at the south-eastern end of Lake Tanganyika, is at Kalambo Falls. It was excavated by Clark. It yielded an interesting stratigraphy, with a series of layers, the latest of which could be dated by Carbon[14] to the Iron Age (1,080 of our era); microlithic Magosian from the Late Stone Age (7550 BC); Upper Lupemban, then Lupemban, similar to that in the Congo, belonging geologically to the Upper Gamblian (last pluvial period), 25 to 27,000 BC; then Sangoan (38 to 41,000 BC); and lastly some layers of very good final Acheulean, dating from about 55,000 years before our era, the last being fully contemporary with West

European Mousterian. The industry includes fine handaxes, cleavers and small flake-tools. And – what is particularly precious – the wood has been partially preserved. There are pieces of bark which may have served as receptacles, longer and shorter pieces of wood, some of them with the bark removed, and sliced off at a slant at one or both ends, which may have been used for digging or may have been the end of a hunting-spear. One of these habitat levels yielded an arc of a stone circle, perhaps marking the base of a branch shelter. In level 5 were found the oldest certain remains of fire known in Africa. This habitat belongs to the Early Gamblian, and must have been occupied in a period of humid climate (see figure 21).

In the Upper Zambesi valley, in northern Rhodesia, Clark has noted the following evolution: Lower Rhodesian Acheulean, with thick handaxes, relatively symmetrical; cleavers on lateral flakes, with both stone hammer and soft hammer retouch; Middle Acheulean, with lanceolate handaxes, oval handaxes, limandes, flake cleavers displaying the technique sometimes known as

*Figure 19* Excavation in the lower layers at Combe-Grenal (Dordogne, France). These layers (Acheulean and Early Mousterian) are situated far outside the present shelter. The roof that protected them collapsed before the Würm I and before the Würm II respectively. Part of this collapsed roof can be seen at the level of the head of the nearest person to the right of the picture. The recent Mousterian layers (see figure 3) are situated over this collapsed roof.

*Tachenghit*, soft hammer retouch; Upper Acheulean, with lanceolate handaxes, pointed handaxes, ovates, limandes especially on flakes, and more evolved U-shaped cleavers.

There is also Acheulean in Ethiopia. In Somaliland the climate after man came on the scene would seem always to have been semi-arid. This area has produced some Upper Acheulean, with signs of Levallois technique, and some cleavers.

In Nubia, in the Sudan, the very fine Acheulean site at Khor Abu Anga, near Khartoum, is presently to be excavated. In the former excavations, more than a thousand handaxes were collected, but only one cleaver and that not a very typical one. At Wadi Afu, in the Southern Sudan, some advanced Acheulean has also been discovered. Recent research by J. Guichard, in the course of expeditions to salvage the Nubian monuments, was especially directed to the surface deposits, which were systematically studied. Using statistical methods, Guichard distinguishes between Lower, Middle and Upper Acheulean, clearly differentiated by the typology and proportions of the handaxes. The Levallois technique crops up in the Middle Acheulean, though the para-Levallois (Victoria-West) technique characteristic of the African Acheulean is absent. There is a notable complete absence of flake cleavers, a feature which clearly distinguishes this Nubian Acheulean from its parallels in the rest of Africa.

In Egypt, the Nile gravels contain some Acheulean at various stages of evolution, but there are no cleavers. The Kharga oasis has provided Miss Caton-Thompson with flake tools at the bottom, then higher up a different Acheulean level containing less refined handaxes but some Levallois flake tools.

At Wanyanga near the Ennedi, in the eastern part of Chad, Arkell has recently found an Acheulean stage very closely akin to the Nubian and likewise without flake cleavers, although there are some European-type cleavers.

In South Africa there is a long tradition of prehistoric research. The stratigraphy of the Vaal Valley is still often used as a basis (figure 23). The Older Gravels extend in two sheets. The basal Older Gravels are sterile; but the Older Red Gravels, which include redeposited basal gravels, contain Oldowan pebble tools, or (according to Mason) Abbevillian implements as well. The Younger Gravels fall into three terraces, in which the evolution of the Abbevillian – Acheulean has been followed though for a long time it was known by the local name of Stellenbosch. The higher terrace of Younger Gravels (twelve metres above bedrock) contains the Early Stellenbosch I (rolled); whilst the second sheet contains Stellenbosch II (rolled), and III and IV (Acheulean). The third sheet (three metres) also contains some Stellenbosch IV. Then come sandy deposits in and under which is Stellenbosch V (Upper Acheulean) and the beginnings of Fauresmith (a kind of Mousterian with an Acheulean tradition). In this series the cores have developed as follows: in stage I, they have no special shape, and the technique is known as 'Clactonian' (flakes with large oblique striking-platform); in stage II (Lower Acheulean), the cores are less shapeless, and the angle of the striking-platform less obtuse; in stage III there are signs of the Victoria-West technique, proto- or para-Levallois. The core has been prepared, but the blow by which the flake has been detached was delivered at the side, thus giving a short broad flake suitable for making flake cleavers. In stage IV the cores become circular and Levallois (Victoria-West II); in stage V they are flatter and clearly semi-circular in form. There has been some discussion as to whether stages IV and V are really separable (see figure 23).

There are traces of some Acheulean occupation in certain caves in South Africa, the Montagu Cave in Western Cape Province, excavated in 1919, having the longest history. It yielded three Acheulean layers, with numerous handaxes, often very fine one (elongated cordiforms, Micoquian forms, lanceolates), cleavers, and

*Figure 20* (*Above*) Flake cleaver from Isimila, in Tanzania (excavations by F. Clark Howell).

*Figure 21* (*Below*) Upper Acheulean handaxes from Kalambo Falls, northern Rhodesia (excavations by Desmond Clark).

*Figure 22* Upper Acheulean handaxes from Isimila, Tanzania.

a quantity of cores and flake-tools. There were no certain traces of fire. The Cave of Hearths in Makapan Valley, in the Transvaal, has produced some Acheulean and later industries, this time with some traces of fire in the Acheulean levels.

In south-west Africa there is no proof of human habitation before a rather late Acheulean. The more abundant rains at the end of the Middle Pleistocene allowed the Acheuleans to penetrate into the Kalahari Desert.

In the southern Congo the Acheulean is poorly represented, as it is in all the high rainfall zones of western and equatorial Africa; and even then it is late Acheulean. The best site is at Kamoa on the watershed between the Zambesi and the Congo. There are ovates and limandes, associated with the U-shaped cleavers, trihedral picks and flake tools. The whole forms an assemblage of the final Acheulean, with shapes that foreshadow the Sangoan.

The Lower Congo contains no Acheulean types, apart from one bifacial tool at Leopoldville. At Brazzaville, large flakes and trihedral picks have been found, perhaps representing ancient industries. In North-Eastern Angola, there have been finds of the Acheulean, also tending towards the Sangoan.

In West Africa, in a 130-kilometre radius round Jos in Nigeria, there are Acheulean-type cleavers in great number. Acheulean abounds in Mali in the sub-Saharan zone. Some sites are very rich in cleavers, but others have none at all. One handaxe has been found at Dakar, one at Pita (Guinea) and Bingerville (Ivory Coast); and recently a rich Acheulean site has been found in Mauritania.

The Casablanca region of Morocco – particularly at Sidi Abderrahman – has yielded a fine sequence of discoveries. After the Oldowan tool-levels come the handaxe industries. This development has been connected with a chronology essentially based upon sea levels and so difficult to link up with other chronologies, in spite of the recent work by Biberson and others. What had been quite unnecessarily called the Clacto-Abbevillian is really Abbevillian, with rough handaxes, sometimes trihedral in shape, spheroid stones, crude cleaver types, flakes, some of them retouched, and still a good number of tools of the Oldowan type. Trihedrons, which are rare in this first stage, develop in the course of stages II and III. Biberson rather misleadingly calls the whole Lower Acheulian. This evolution continues through the Moroccan Middle Acheulean (stages IV to VII). The handaxes become more varied in shape, the trihedrons disappear, the cleavers vary in proportion, and flake tools develop. There are cores of the Victoria-West type for obtaining short broad flakes suitable for transforming into handaxes and cleavers, and some Levallois cores. Pebble tools continue to occur. The fully evolved Acheulean comprises the following stages: Stage VII, with fine well-made handaxes, lanceolate or ovate, not many cleavers, very abundant flakes and flake tools (points and scrapers), and cores frequently of the Levallois type. Then in stage VIII, the handaxes tend towards the Mousterian type, being cordiform and definitely smaller, or subtriangular, although there is a continuance of lanceolate handaxes of the Upper Acheulean type, and sometimes cleavers as well as pebble tools. There are numerous flake tools, and some Levallois or discoid cores. Stage VIII as a whole gives the impression of Mousterian of Acheulean tradition, and is certainly very late.

There is a very important deposit at Ternifine (also called Palikao) in Algeria, 22 kilometres east of Mascara. This would seem to be an ancient Acheulean level, contemporary to Acheulean I or II at Casablanca, where pebble tools play a great part. The cleavers are primitive in type, and the handaxes generally rough. There may however be several Acheulean levels represented in this ancient source, since the deposit is one to five metres thick. While excavating, Arambourg found several Pithecanthropus mandibles

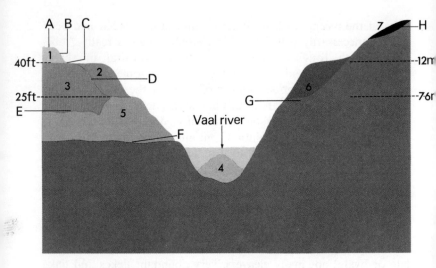

*Figure 23* Cross-section of the Vaal Valley, following Van Riet Lowe. 1 and 2, Red Sands; 3, calcified sands; 4, Younger Gravels 3; 5, Younger Gravels 2a and b; 6, Younger Gravels 1; 7, Older Gravels; A, Later Stone Age; B, Middle Stone Age; C, Lower Fauresmithian; D, Upper Fauresmithian; E, Final Acheulean; F and G, Acheulean; H, 'pebble culture' and 'Chellean'.

(*Atlanthropus mauritanicus*).

Near Tlemcen, there is another spring deposit, called Lake Karar, which has also yielded some rather primitive Acheulean types. But the discoveries at El Ma el Abiod, thirty kilometres south of Tebessa, produced very different material – a splendid Final Acheulean with finely-made handaxes, lanceolate or cordiform, but no cleavers. It resembles the Micoquian at Sidi-Zin in Tunisia. This deposit, near Kef in Western Tunisia, contains three layers excavated by Dr Gobert, The industry is usually flaked out of white limestone. The lowest level has yielded chipped pebbles, Oldowan in type, but often more evolved, lanceolate or Micoquian handaxes, cordiforms and elongated cordiforms, and flake tools but no cleavers. The middle layer is very different: it contains no lanceolate handaxes, but only elongated cordiforms and a good number of typical cleavers, as well as 'unifacial handaxes', made from large flakes, of which only the upper surface has

*Figure 24* Map of Eastern Africa showing the main Lower and Middle Palaeolithic sites.

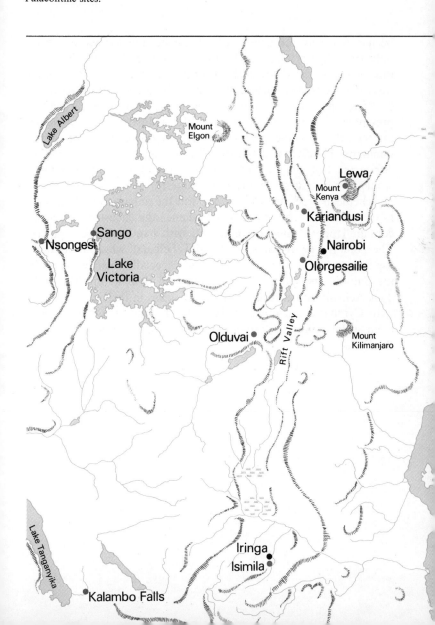

been extensively retouched, whilst the bottom surface has been only very slightly trimmed by the removal of the bulb. Tools of this type are common in the French Acheulean of Mousterian tradition. To these industrial finds must be added various scrapers, etc. The upper level is a repetition of the lower one. So we are presented with two clearly differentiated industries, one surrounding the other. Do these represent two separate cultures, or simply remnants of different activities? The existence of large zones in Africa (such as Egypt and Nubia) where cleavers are unknown would rather suggest the former hypothesis.

Acheulean types are widely found in the Sahara, and often in a fairly evolved form. At Erg Tihodaïne, the lacustrine deposits contain Upper Acheulean material, with handaxes and cleavers. The same is true of Tachenghit and Tabelbalat, which are famous for the beauty of their handaxes and especially their cleavers. In the Sahara, the latter are more plentiful than in the Maghreb. This Acheulean with cleavers is found again in the Fezzan.

In Cyrenaica the Lower Palaeolithic is only known at present from surface finds. In Tripolitania, one might mention the site at Bir Dufan.

In Asia, bifacial industries are definitely less widespread than in Europe or Africa (with the exception of the Middle East and India; see figure 25).

In Israel, we have already looked at the deposit at Ubeidyia, above the Jordan Valley, probably belonging rather to the cycle of handaxe industries than to the Oldowan. Not many of the Palestine deposits have yielded Lower or Middle Acheulean. Upper Acheulean material being more widespread, one might mention the valley of Rephaim-Baqua at Jerusalem. At Banat Yaqoub as well as handaxes there are cleavers of an African type. Acheulean is also found in caves in Jordania, Israel and Syria. The cave at Oum Qatafa in the Judaean desert was excavated by R. Neuville. At the bottom it contains a rough industry without handaxes, attributed to the Tayacian (see below). Above this there is what has been called Middle Acheulean, but this really seems to belong to the Upper with amygdaliform or lanceolate handaxes, side scrapers, burins, etc. Over it comes the Upper Acheulean, which to start with differs little from the Middle; but then it becomes plentiful in Micoquian style handaxes, accompanied by flake tools, sometimes on Levallois flakes, among which there are various scrapers and gravers.

In Israel, the Mount Carmel cave at El Tabun, excavated by Miss Garrod, also yielded at the lowest level an industry without handaxes, which is then followed by Acheulean types which seem to include towards the top a layer with a curious blade industry. At Jabrud in Syria, excavated by A. Rust, there is some Upper Acheulean material interstratified with a flake industry, known as the Jabrudian, which is reminiscent of the Quina-type Mousterian, but is rich in asymmetrical scrapers (Winkelkratzers), and has on top of it this blade industry (pre-Aurignacian). It should be noted that none of these sites has yielded flake cleavers. The age of this cave – Acheulean is debatable; it could be very late, like the final North

African Acheulean, and might belong to the Würm glaciation.

In south-eastern Anatolia (Turkey) there are remains of what would seem to be a final Acheulean, and some traces of it have been recently discovered on the shores of the Bosphorus.

In Armenia, south of the Caucasus, there is the deposit at Satani-Dar in the Aragatz massif, at an altitude of 1,600 metres. It is a surface site where there are said to have been found some Abbevillian and Acheulean obsidian tools.

In the centre of the Caucasus, in southern Ossetia, there is the Laché-Balta deposit, which – to judge by the handaxes – appears to be of a fairly early Acheulean stage, although there are some Levallois flakes. There has also been found in the Caucasus at an altitude of 1,700 metres some 'Middle' Acheulean – according to the stratigraphy – in the Koudaro cave beneath some Mousterian. It has produced typical handaxes and fairly refined flake tools, and there are specimens of the Levallois-type débitage. In Trans-caucasia, the Azykhskaya cave, more than 1,400 metres in altitude, has also produced some 'Middle' Acheulean. It seems difficult to believe that caves situated at that height could have been occupied during the Riss glaciation, and this must probably belong to the interglacial Upper Acheulean. The Acheulean has also been noted in Arabia. It probably exists too in Iran and Afghanistan, but the great Asiatic centre for it is the Indian Peninsula. According to the findings of H. de Terra, Movius and others, and the more recent research of Indian and Pakistani archaeologists, it would seem that this peninsula falls into two zones: a southern and central zone where handaxe industries predominate, and a north-western area where they are less numerous and where industries without hand-axes developed.

In the Potwar district of the Punjab, Abbevillian – Acheulian types are dated to the second Himalayan Interglacial and the third ice-age. The most important site is at Chauntra in the Soan valley.

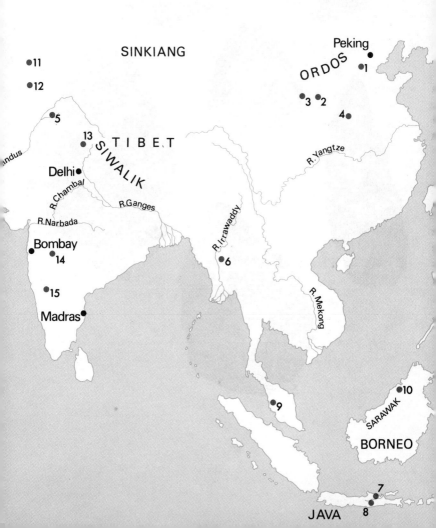

*Figure 25* Position of some Asiatic palaeolithic sites. 1, Choukoutien; 2, Sjara-osso-gol; 3, Shui-tung-kou; 4, Tingtsun; 5, Soan; 6, Irrawadi sites; 7, Trinil; 8, Padjitan; 9, Kota Tampan; 10, Nyah Cave; 11, Teshik-Tash and Aman-Kutan region; 12, Kara-Kamar; 13, Beas and Bananga Rivers; 14, Priavada river; 15, Malaprahba river.

79

*Figure 26* Padjitanian tools
from Padjitan (Java).
1, chopping tool; 2,3, two
rough scrapers; 4, handaxe;
5, pick; 6, pointed scraper.

Paterson divided the finds into three groups, according to their physical state: first, those that were much rolled and abraded, which included the Abbevillian handaxes and some flakes; then a second group, less worn, comprising the Lower and Middle Acheulean; and finally a third group, quite fresh, of Upper or evolved Middle Acheulean type, with discoid cores and more or less typical Levallois flakes.

Three hundred kilometres north of Delhi, the terraces of the Beas and Banganga Rivers have yielded a series of Lower Palaeolithic finds with a large number of pebble tools, handaxes and flake cleavers of African type. South of Delhi, in Rajasthan, the lower gravels of the River Chambal have produced Acheulean handaxes and flake cleavers; the Gambhiri basin some Abbevillian – Acheulean pebble tools and cleavers; and the River Shivna a more evolved Acheulean material, also with cleavers. The Narmada (or Narbada) Valley in Central India has produced in the lower gravels of its terraces some Abbevillian handaxes, rough choppers, and non-descript flakes; and in the superimposed clay, Acheulean handaxes and cleavers with proto-Levallois flakes. 200 kilometres to the east of Bombay, the gravels of the Pravada have yielded evolved Abbevillian and Middle Acheulean industries with cleavers. The Madras district has long been known for its Middle Acheulean industry. In the Malaprahba basin, Southern India, there is some Middle and Upper Acheulean with very fine evolved cleavers, chopping-tools and flakes, some of which are Levallois. Some of the long-shaped handaxes are reminiscent of the Sangoan picks.

Apart from perhaps a few isolated handaxes here and there in China, the only place in south-eastern Asia outside India where a clearly-defined handaxe industry occurs appears to be Java, in the Padjitan region on the southern coast. There have been surface finds of numerous tools of the Lower Palaeolithic type. According to Movius, there are no true handaxes here, and this industry would belong to the complex with no handaxes that we shall be considering later. But it seems to us, on the contrary, that it does contain entirely characteristic handaxes, and if they had been found in India they would unhesitatingly have been classed as Acheulean. It should be noted that some of them tend towards the Sangoan pick. There are also some big planes, and flake tools that are sometimes of the Levallois type (see figure 26).

The Trinil layers, with their *Homo* (*Pithecanthropus*) *erectus* remains, are also recently said to have produced some tools.

# 7 Lower Palaeolithic industries without handaxes

It is undoubtedly true that the Lower Palaeolithic contained industries without handaxes. Obermaier, and then Breuil, had long been calling attention to the rarity of 'coups de poing' (handaxes) in Central and Eastern Europe. If sometimes, in zones where there are usually plenty of handaxes, their absence may only indicate a workshop or places where specialised activities did not require handaxes, in vast tracts of the Old World these industries without handaxes exist alone, and in other parts are sufficiently distinct from the Abbevillian - Acheulean types to be recognised as a separate class. Breuil had differentiated between three flake industries: the Clactonian, the Tayacian and the Levalloisian. The last was based upon a mistaken interpretation of the sequences of Somme Valley terraces and industries. Contrary to what he supposed, there is no industry with Levallois flakes and without handaxes contemporary with the Middle and Upper Acheulean. In France as in Africa the Levallois technique appears in Middle Acheulean and develops in the Upper. The term Tayacian, as we shall see, probably covers different things and should at least be redefined. The Clactonian was for a long time characterised simply and solely by a particular production technique in which large flakes with plain sloping platforms were obtained by striking on an anvil; but it has really made good its status as an independent industry as a result of Hazzledine Warren's researches at Clacton, and also through the discovery of a widespread flake and chopper tool complex occupying a large part of Asia, and probably Europe and the East as well. As one can only understand the European problems in the light of data furnished by Asia, it is with the latter that we will begin.

In the Soan region of the Punjab, in the north-west of the Indian Peninsula, there is a flake and chopper tool industry known as Soan. A series of large, thick, massive flakes, with broad plain platforms called the Pre-Soan is dated to the second Himalayan glaciation.

84

*Figure 27* Tools from the Sinanthropus
beds at Choukoutien. 1, small chopping-
tool from locality 13; 2, Levallois-
like flake; 3, point; 4, chopper (locality 1);
5, cleaver-like tool (locality 15).

The Early Soan (figure 29, 4, 5, 6) falls within the Second Himalayan
interglacial period. It possesses pebble tools closely reminiscent of
the Oldowan, worked either unifacially or bifacially, and sometimes pointed. In the evolved Early Soan there is the addition of
flakes and cores of the proto-Levallois type. The Upper Soan is
dated contemporary with the Riss glaciation, or rather the third
Himalayan glaciation. It is very widespread in the Punjab, and still
possesses some pebble tools, but especially flake tools, often
obviously Levalloisian, as are the cores.

China, apart perhaps from one or two isolated handaxes, has
only produced industries of this chopping-tool group. The principal site is clearly the one at Choukoutien (figure 28), probably
going back in its principal sites to the Mindelian or perhaps
Mindel/Riss Interglacial. It lies some forty kilometres from Peking
and was made famous by the discovery of numerous Sinanthropus
skeletal remains (*Pithecanthropus Pekinensis* or *Homo erectus
Pekinensis*). The site that has produced the most ancient traces of
human industry is Locality 13, with a small and rather shapeless
chopping-tool, and some charcoal. Site I (the most important) is a
little later, and contains the deposits, some fifty metres thick, which
yielded the Sinanthropus remains. The cave deposits are composed
of limestone debris, ash and contain fauna, and human artifacts,
which show no great typological difference from the bottom to the
top. This industry is often amorphous, and made up of quartz flakes
detached by bipolar working, i.e. the core was placed on an anvil
when struck, giving a bulb of percussion at both ends of the flake.
But these shapeless flakes are accompanied by artifacts of a better
and sometimes surprisingly good quality. There are choppers and
chopping tools, and flake implements which include small scrapers,
sometimes convergent, and various other pieces. Towards the top
there are some larger and better-made scrapers (see figure 27,
1 to 4).

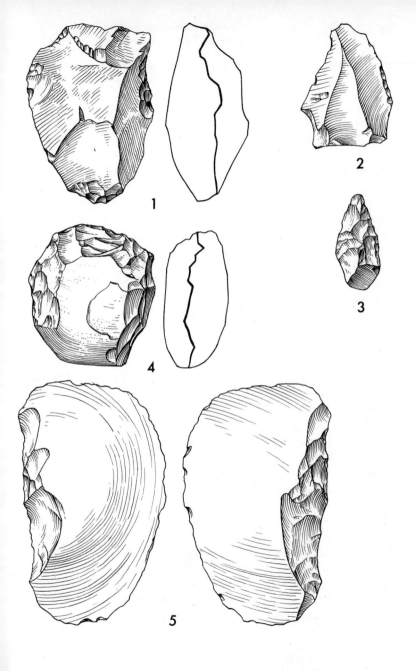

*Figure 28* General view from the north
of locality 1 at Choukoutien. The Chinese
name is Lungkushan (Dragon Bone Hill). Many
fossiliferous sites in China have been exploited for
'dragon bones' used in the Chinese pharmacopeia.

Locality 15 is definitely later, and is often attributed to the Riss Glaciation. Taken as a whole, the implements are like those at Locality 1, but of better quality. These are elongated choppers and chopping tools, reminiscent in outline of a handaxe worked only on one edge. Others are classic in type in not being pointed. Among the flake tools, there are some large flakes with the striking platform removed by retouching, resulting in chopping implements that are not cleavers in the Acheulean sense but which may have been used for the same purpose (see figure 27, 5). Some of the flakes come from prepared cores and take on a Levallois look, but these are very rare. There are scrapers, sometimes made from small pebbles, transverse scrapers, and small leaf-shaped tools, sometimes bifacial.

Recently archaeological layers have been discovered under the classical layers of Locality 1, apparently contemporary with Locality 13.

The Fenho complex in Shansi and Honan provinces is often thought to fill the gap between Choukoutien and Chinese 'Mousterian'. The implements include some carefully flaked stone balls, large tools more or less bifacially worked, and pebble tools often worked on both faces; but flake tools preponderate and bipolar working is absent, which may be due to the use of a material that does not require this technique. The flake tools include scrapers, pointed flakes, flat discs, etc. (see figure 29, 1,2,3).

When this Fenho complex is better known it will no doubt have to be subdivided, for there is a great deal of typological variety in assemblages that are broadly speaking contemporary. In various places there have been finds of bifacial tools, and from near Tingtsun there has even come a description of 'a typical Acheulean handaxe' found on the surface. There were also found at this same point, but in situ with artifacts from the Fenho complex, some teeth which were morphologically intermediate between the *Sinanthropus* and modern man. This complex, as far as the ancient

forms are concerned, is generally dated to the Riss glacial or to the Riss/Würm Interglacial – contemporary, that is, with Locality 15 in the Choukoutien site, with which it shows marked affinities.

In Burma, the Irrawaddy Valley terraces have yielded an industry known as Anyathian (figure 29, 7, 8) composed of artifacts of either silicified wood – which is not at all easily flaked – or silicified tuffs, which is a better material. A distinction has been made – according to the stratigraphical position – between an Early Anyathian and a Late Anyathian phase, though there is not much difference in the typology, the first being attributed to the second pluvial, second interpluvial and third pluvial, whilst the Late phase would belong to the third interpluvial and fourth pluvial. In the Early Anyathian, the silicified wood gives a monotonous typology to the implements: choppers, sometimes pointed. The tools made of silicified tuff are more varied, and comprised of unifacial and bifacial tools of the Oldowan type, as well as occasional flakes that have been retouched to form scrapers. The Late Anyathian includes essentially the same

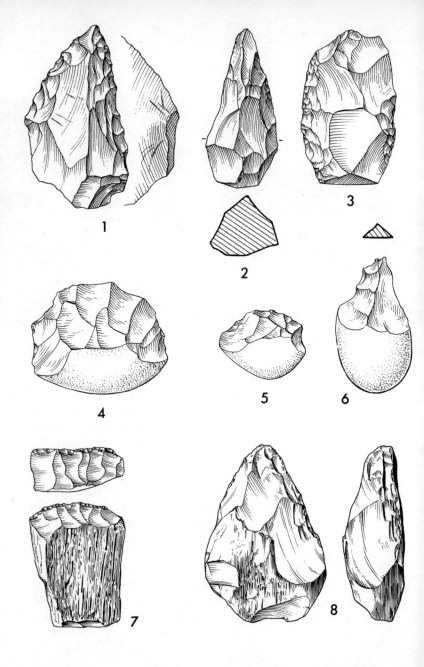

*Figure 29* Palaeolithic tools from Tingtsun (China). **89**
1, scraper; 2, pick; 3, scraper. Tools from the Lower
Soanian (northern India). 4,5, choppers; 6, pointed chopper.
Tools from the Anyathian (Burma). 7, chopper made of
silicified wood; 8, pointed chopper made of silicified tuff.


types but without chopping-tools. The flakes seem to have been
prepared before being struck from the cores, but they have un-
facetted platforms.

In Malaysia, Movius associates the finds made near Kota
Tampan (Tampanian) in northern Malaysia on the River Perak
with the group of chopper-industries. It seems there are both
choppers and chopping tools, but also some rough handaxes, and
this industry is perhaps akin to that of Padjitan in Java.

In Thailand there is a pebble tool industry, but its age is as yet
undetermined.

It would seem, then, to be a well-established fact that south-
eastern Asia contains a great industrial complex that has evolved
differently from the bifacial complex. But this complex probably
sent out feelers far to the west, by a route that is as yet imperfectly
understood but which may have passed through the south of the
Soviet Union. On the shore of the Sea of Azov, near Taganrog,
the site of Gherasimovka has yielded a chopping tool and scrapers
from some ancient – perhaps even Pre-Mindelian – levels.

At the site of Vérteszöllös in Hungary, Vértes and Kretzoi
have described an industry that I myself have been able to see. The
fauna suggests a Mindel interstadial date. The site is fifty kilometres west of Budapest, in deposits of travertine (Calcareous
Spring deposits) and loess. This industry comprises more than
3,000 tools and flakes, but contains no handaxes. Nearly all the
tools and flakes are fabricated from pebbles. The implements –
especially those in quartz and flint – are very small, averaging only
2·5 centimetres in length. The smallest flake tool measures eleven
millimetres and the largest sixty-two millimetre. Among these
miniature tools there are typical choppers and chopping-tools, the
latter sometimes developing a bifacial point. Along with these there
are some very small scrapers of various types with a very fine
retouch, which it is surprising to find at this level. There are also

*Figure 30* Choppers and flake tools
from Vértesszöllös in Hungary (enlarged).

*Figure 31* Flint tools from Clacton (England). 1, end-scraper; 2, 5, 'Bill-hooks', 3, denticulate tool; 4, side-scraper; 6, flint chopping-tool. These chopping-tools made from flint nodules had been mistaken for cores.

denticulated tools, Clactonian notched scrapers, made by a single blow and sometimes also end-scrapers and atypical borers. Burnt bones show that fire was used; and quite recently, teeth have been found in the layer, and a Pithecanthropus occipital bone. There is a similar site at Budapest itself (see figure 30).

The Czechoslovakian finds represent a more recent stage, and their scantiness may leave room for a good deal of discussion. In Poland there have been discoveries of 'Clactonian' flake tools in the Early Riss deposits.

In France there are various deposits which seem to belong to the complex of industries with choppers and chopping-tools but no handaxes. The cave at Pech de l'Aze II in the Dordogne has produced in layers of Early Riss date a non-handaxe industry which possesses pebble-tools akin to the Clactonian. It is probable that Fontéchevade in the Charente also belongs to this period, in spite of what is called a 'warm' fauna, which also exists at Pech de l'Aze, and its industry is probably Clactonian and 'Tayacian'. At Sainte-Anne-d'Evenos in Provence, E. Bonifay and H. de Lumley found an open-air site which produced an industry probably of Riss date and of the same type.

But the key deposit is in England, at Clacton on the Essex coast. For a long time the definition adopted for this industry has been almost purely technical, founded upon the characteristics of the flake as given by Breuil: flaked by the anvil technique with a broad striking-platform making a very wide angle with the flake-face; a very well-marked and often multiple percussion cone, and strong ripple-marks in the flake surface; a globular core; no handaxes. This is much too broad a definition, equally suiting certain flint-knapping workshops in the Neolithic period, and its application has resulted in seeing Clactonian everywhere. From the chronological point of view, Breuil espoused a strange theory which placed the handaxe industries during the interglacial periods, and the flake

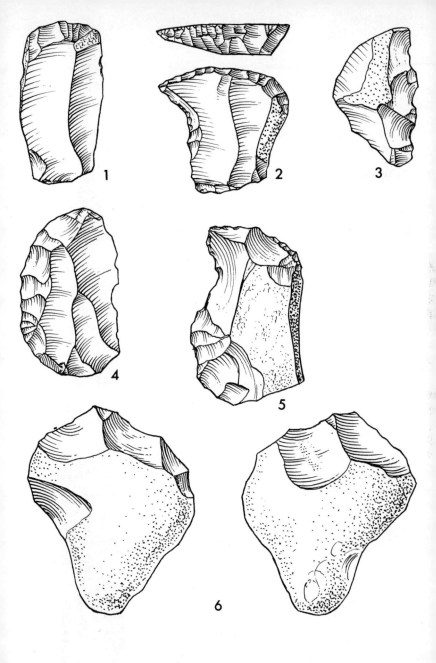

*Figure 32.* Broken wooden spear from the Clactonian. This sharpened fragment of wood, very probably a hunting spear, is one of the very rare wooden Palaeolithic implements to have been preserved.

industries, beginning with the Clactonian, during the glacials. For Breuil, the Clactonian began 'before the Mindel Glaciation' and continued during the ensuing glaciation; and finally, by an obscure and unexplained process, it was transformed into Levalloisian, with flakes of a Levallois type, and into 'Tayacian', with flakes sometimes of the Levallois and sometimes of non-Levallois type.

Warren's patient research at Clacton has made it possible to understand what the Clactonian really is. It is an industry belonging to the non-handaxe line, but in which the choppers and chopping-tools, instead of being fashioned from pebbles, are made from flint nodules and so have been confused with cores. It also contains pebble tools made from quartzite. The flake tools are varied, and the famous 'Clactonian flakes' are probably only the first flakes taken from large nodules.

The choppers and chopping-tools are varied, and sometimes pointed; the flake tools include a variety of scrapers, some side-scrapers reminiscent of the Acheulean types from the Commont workshop, some truncated flakes, a fair number of denticulates and some notches among which there is a special type sometimes also met with elsewhere, but which is characteristic of the Clactonian. It is obtained by detaching a small single flake, and gives a concave cutting edge. Warren also calls attention to a special tool, the 'bill-hook', with a lateral Clactonian notch near the end of the flake, which has a transverse truncation (figures 31 and 32). The un-retouched flakes are of various types, sometimes almost Levallois, although the striking-platforms are usually smooth. Interestingly, the point of a wooden hunting-spear has been found at Clacton. The age of the Clacton finds is a matter of debate. The estimates vary from the Mindel to the end of the Mindel/Riss.

Often linked up with the evolved Clactonian is the industry at High Lodge, near Mildenhall. This industry, which probably belongs to a Rissian interstadial, is definitely more refined. It is of large dimensions, and the quality of the retouching is striking. Scrapers largely predominate, either lateral or transversal, and often convex, with stepped, fish-scale-like retouch, similar to the Mousterian Quina type. Others are double, convergent, or canted. There are some good end-scrapers, recalling those in the Commont workshop. In the collections coming from the older excavations there are no Oldowan-type tools; but this is of no great significance, for only the finer objects would seem to have been collected. New excavations are now proceeding and will perhaps change the interpretation put upon this site.

A few kilometres from Les Eyzies (Dordogne), the deposits at La Micoque deserve some attention. Here, under a layer of Micoquan (or final Acheulean) belonging to the Würm glaciation, is the last interglacial soil, then layer 5, which has been ascribed to the Tayacian. In reality it contains some Acheulean-type handaxes, and is probably Acheulean. Layer 4 contains a large quantity of flat flake tools, sometimes Levallois in type, and hardly differs from an early typical Mousterian. Layer 3 has some resemblances – apart from the dimensions of the tools – with the High Lodge Clactonian and so with a primitive Quina-type Mousterian. It also includes some flint chopping-tools. These two layers had been ascribed to the 'Tayacian'; and it may therefore be asked whether there is any good reason for the existence of this term, unless it be to designate either an evolved Clactonian, or a possible ancestor of Mousterian, or both. In Layer 2 the implements have been completely crushed by cryoturbation, and it is no longer possible to say anything about them, any more than about the crushed industries which have been found in between layers 3, 4 and 5. All these layers are certainly Rissian. Layer 1 only exists in the form of blocks of breccia in a derived position. It is very poor in remains and dates perhaps from the Mindel glaciation; only a few flakes have been found from it.

In the Rigabe cave in Provence, Bonifay discovered in the

Rissian layers an industry that appears, like Layer 4 of La Micoque, to be Early Mousterian. There are also industries more or less linked up with the older layers of La Micoque in the Baume–Bonne cave at Quinson, as one comes out of the Verdon gorges in Provence (excavated by Bottet and De Lumley). The presence of typical handaxes suggests, however, that it may simply be an Acheulean facies which is poor in handaxes.

In Germany, at Ehringsdorf near Weimar, in the travertines of the last interglacial period, there is an industry that also appears to be an Early Mousterian tending towards the Quina-Ferrassie type, with some 'oriental' peculiarities.

At Kiik-Koba in the Crimea the lower layers have been compared with the lower layers of La Micoque, and there are in fact some typological resemblances.

# 8 The Mousterian stage in Europe

Under the term Mousterian stage, we shall consider industries extending over the whole surface of the ancient world that are of different ages but all belonging to the Würm glaciation. Although they often present striking marks of originality, they have this much in common, that they are at a certain technical and typological level which may be reached earlier or later according to the particular locality. This level was in fact already reached – or almost reached – by certain older industries, such as the one at Rigabe, contemporary to Layer 4 of La Micoque or at Ehringsdorf. It is always artificial to subdivide a continuously evolving process.

In Europe, then, the Mousterian has roots that go down to the last interglacial or even to the Rissian glaciation. And from the beginning of the last glaciation, we find it in various forms over the whole extent of Europe. It is in fact being increasingly realised that the Mousterian is a composite or complex of industries rather than any specific one, and the typological differences, no less than the probably differing origins, prevent us from considering these various Mousterian traits as simple facies.

The Mousterians have left numerous traces of their cultures in shelters and cave-entrances, on the plateaux and in the valleys, and even on the loess plains, though in France they seem only to have occupied these in the periods of relatively mild climate. They even penetrated the mountains, but these probably only in the inter-glacial or interstadial periods. Whatever the circumstances, there were powerful human groups living in Europe at this time, and their supremacy was to extend into the first two stages of the last glaciation (the first stage, according to the Central European classification).

In France there are various types of Mousterian, the most important of which are as follows: 1 *Typical Mousterian:* (see (figure 33). This derives probably from an industry such as that in Layer 4 at La Micoque or that of the Rigabe Rissian layers. To

*Figure 33* Flint implements of the typical Mousterian.
1, convex side-scraper; 2, Levallois point; 3,4,5, Mousterian points;
6, canted scraper; 7, transversal scraper; 8, convergent scraper; 9, double
scraper; 10, Levallois flake. (Combe-Grenal, Dordogne, layer 29, except 2,
from Houppeville, Normandy, and 10, from Corbiac, Dordogne.)

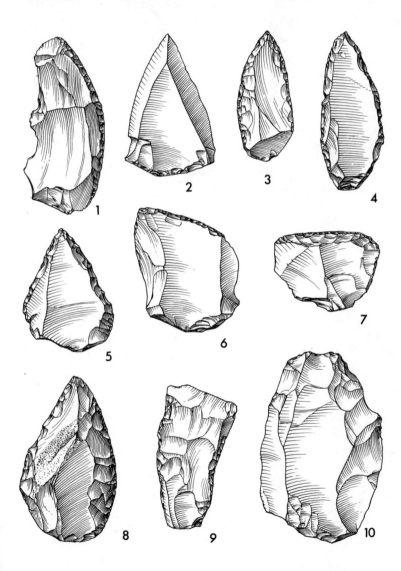

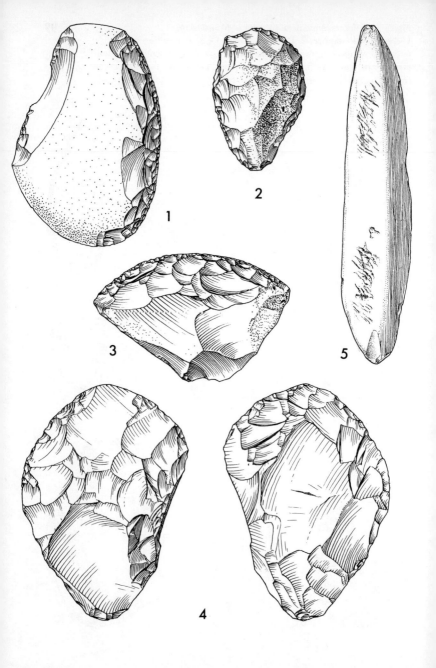

1

2

3

5

4

*Figure 34* Tools from the Quina-type Mousterian.
1, convex side-scraper; 2, thick end and
side-scraper; 3, transversal scraper, Quina-type;
4, bifacial scraper, Quina-type; 5, bone retoucher.
(Combe-Grenal, Dordogne, layer 23.)

varying extents it also uses the Levallois technique. Only in exceptional cases does it contain handaxes (assuming that those attributed to it do really belong to it); and its percentage of scrapers varies from twenty-five to fifty-five. Points are well developed and carefully worked. Limaces (double pointed scrapers retouched all round) are rare; there are very few or no backed knives, and notched flakes and denticulates only make up a relatively small percentage. The Neanderthal man found at Le Moustier belonged to this type of Mousterian, and not to the Mousterian of Acheulean tradition, as is often believed. The typical Mousterian is present from the beginning of Würm I and lasts on to the end of Würm II.
2 *The Quina-Ferrassie* or Charentian-type Mousterian (see figure 34), named after its predominance in the Charente. It is probably derived from a High Lodge type of industry, or from Layer 3 at La Micoque, through the intermediary of industries of the Ehringsdorf type. The Quina type Mousterian always includes a very high percentage of scrapers (fifty to eighty per cent). It comprises a good number of special scrapers, which are rare or completely lacking in the other Mousterian phases: simple thick scrapers, decidedly convex, and with scalariform retouch, numerous transverse scrapers retouched in the same way; scrapers with bifacial retouch some-times over the whole surface (*tranchoirs*), representing no doubt the final evolution of the chopping-tool, and some limaces. There are some end-scrapers, often with a tendency towards the carinate or nosed form; few or no handaxes, and those which do occur are of a pyriform shape; no backed knives, but fairly numerous notched flakes, often of the Clactonian type; relatively few denticulates, except towards the end. The technique is non-Levallois, the flakes are short and thick, often with a plain striking-platform. However there are sometimes some fine Levallois flakes.

The Ferrassie-type Mousterian seems to be a simple facies of the preceding type. The general characteristics are identical, but the

*Figure 35* Denticulate Mousterian tools. 1, side-scraper; 2, 3, 4, Clactonian notches; 5, 7, 8, 11, 13, denticulate tools; 6, knife with natural back; 9, Tayac point; 10, broken tip of a point made of reindeer antler; 12, borer; 14, bola stone. (Combe-Grenal, Dordogne, layer 14, except 10, layer 16.)

typology is somewhat modified by the Levallois technique. As the Levallois flakes are usually long and flat, there are thus fewer transverse scrapers and thick scrapers.

This Mousterian culture also covers the first two Würmian stages. Towards the end of Würm ii, it tends to include more denticulates and so return to its starting-point (Layer 3 of La Micoque). It is to this industry that the greater part of the Neanderthal human remains in western Europe belong (La Quina, La Chapelle aux Saints, La Ferrassie, Le Régourdou, Spy etc.). 3 *Denticulate Mousterian*, the origin of which is at present unknown, appears at the very beginning of the Würm glaciation and continues until practically the end of Würm ii. Its characteristics are mainly negative: no typical handaxes, no typical backed knives, few or no points, few scrapers (five to twenty-five per cent, though very rarely as much as the latter figure), and very mediocre in quality. On the other hand, a great development of denticulated tools (from thirty-five to fifty-five per cent) and of notched flakes. The technique may or may not be Levallois. There are no human remains known from this culture (see figure 35). 4 *The Mousterian of Acheulean tradition* presents two facies which are evolutionary, since the second is always above the first when they are together.

The Mousterian of Acheulean tradition type A (see figure 36) occurs from the beginning of the Würm, and probably even a little earlier. Its numerous handaxes (from eight to forty per cent, but more often ten to fifteen per cent) show it to belong to the Acheulean tradition. They are either triangular (especially at the beginning), often cordiform or subcordiform, or there are sometimes also Upper Acheulean lanceolate types but with a flat instead of a thick butt. It does not seem to be directly derived from the Micoquian, which is partly contemporary with it. The flake tools, which are extremely varied, include a moderate number of scrapers (twenty to forty per cent), very rarely thick in section, and often shaped from

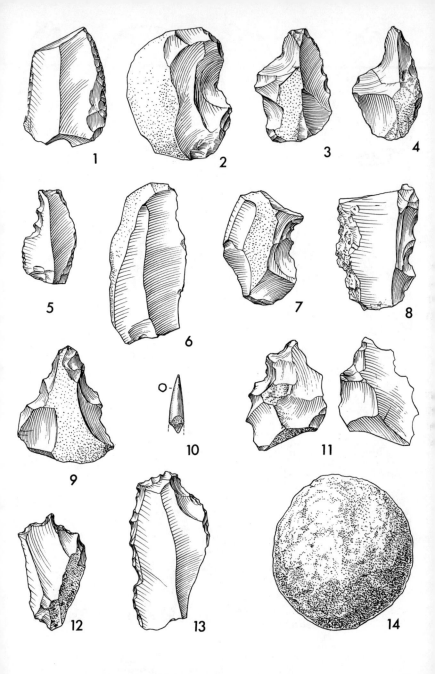

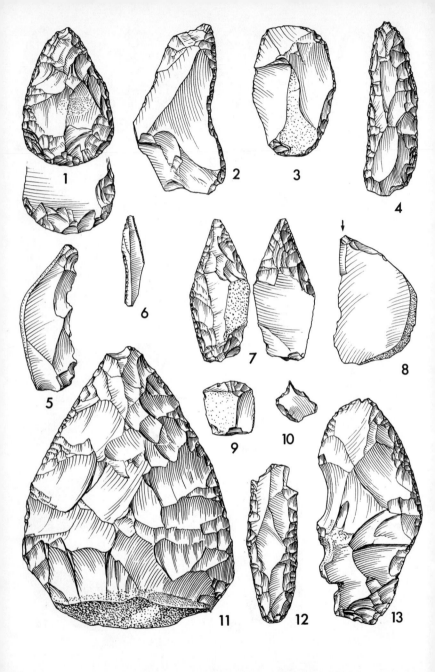

*Figure 36* Mousterian of Acheulean tradition, type A. 1, point with a 105
thinned butt; 2, concave scraper; 3, backed knife; 4, 12, double scrapers
on blades; 5, denticulated tool; 6, bladelet with a small retouch; 7, bifacial
point; 8, burin; 9, short end-scraper; 10, small borer; 11, cordiform
handaxe; 13, convex side-scraper. (All from Pech de l'Azé, lower layer.)

the flakes obtained in making handaxes and retouched by parallel flaking with a soft hammer, like the handaxes. Fairly frequently the retouching is on the lower surface of the flake. There are a number of points, sometimes with thinned butts, sometimes partly bifacial, some notched flakes, fairly numerous and carefully-worked denticulates, some tools of Upper Palaeolithic type (burins, end-scrapers, borers, flakes, and truncated blades) in appreciably larger proportions than in the other types of Mousterian, and finally backed knives, most often in the shape of quadrangular flakes (Abri Audi knives) mostly in fairly small percentages.

Type B is rather different. There are few handaxes (two to eight per cent, often only four to five per cent), often small and of crude workmanship; few side-scrapers (four to ten per cent) and mediocre in quality; but there is a great development of denticulates and especially of backed knives, which are now fashioned on elongated flakes or even on blades and resemble the Chatelperron Early Upper Palaeolithic knife. The other tools of Upper Palaeolithic type develop likewise, and already there are occasionally some double burins (see figure 37).

Between these two types there is in certain deposits, such as Le Pech de l'Azé I, a transitional type. This evolution seems to have come about at the beginning of Würm II. Type B continues until towards the intermediate stage Würm II/III and gives rise to the Lower Perigordian, which is thus indigenous in origin. In border-line cases, it is sometimes difficult to attribute a particular industry to final Acheulean-tradition Mousterian rather than to Early Perigordian. The type of man responsible for the Mousterian of Acheulean tradition is for the moment unknown even if various remains have been mistakenly attributed to him (at Spy, Le Moustier, La Chaise, and Le Pech de l'Azé, which really belong to other industries). This tradition is likewise a western form of Mousterian, which hardly extends beyond the borders of France

*Figure 37* Mousterian of Acheulean tradition, type B. 1, bad point, more or less bifacially worked; 2, backed knife on a blade, foreshadowing the Chatelperron knives of the early Upper Palaeolithic; 3, denticulated and truncated flake; 4, backed knife on a flake; 5, denticulated tool; 6, core for the production of bladelets; 7, borer; 8, 11, small handaxe; 9, end-scraper; 10, double burin. (All from Pech de l'Azé, upper layers.)

except at one or two points.

The name of Alpine Mousterian has been given to some poor collections of remains found in caves at high altitudes all over Europe, often crushed by cryoturbation. It does not really look as if this alpine Mousterian was a separate culture; it probably represents the traces of remains left behind at halting-places during hunting (chiefly of the bear).

In south-western France, the Mousterian with flake cleavers of Spanish type has penetrated rather weakly as far as the Dordogne and more decisively into the French Basque country. (It is known as Vasconian.)

Micoquian is a final Acheulean which has reached the Mousterian stage by virtue of its chronological position – usually in the Würm period – and of its typological development. In the north of France, it is often found at the bottom of younger loess. At La Micoque it is fully Würmian, and separated from the interglacial soil by sterile breccia. Although it must have existed during the last interglacial, it also can be classed as a Würm I industry.

It is characterised by lanceolate handaxes, with a regional variation in size. The butts of these handaxes are fairly globular and these tools often have concave edges, in which case they are called Micoquian type. Along with these handaxes there are cordiform types, often also with fairly thick butts. The rest of the implements are hardly distinguishable from Mousterian of Acheulean tradition type A. The Micoquian may or may not make use of the Levallois technique; if not – as at La Micoque – it sometimes contains thick scrapers of the Quina type (see figure 41).

In England, Mousterian of Acheulean tradition is mainly known from isolated handaxes found on the surface. The site of Baker's Hole may perhaps belong to it; but it may also be Acheulean. In Belgium there was some Quina-type Mousterian (which produced the skeletons) and some Mousterian of Acheulean

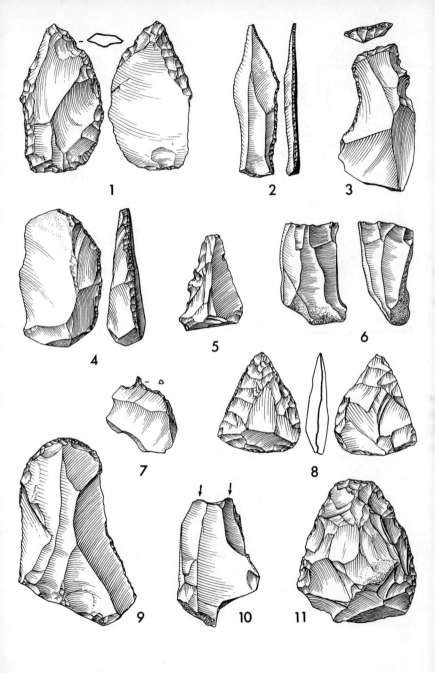

1               2            3

4         5           6

7          8

9        10        11

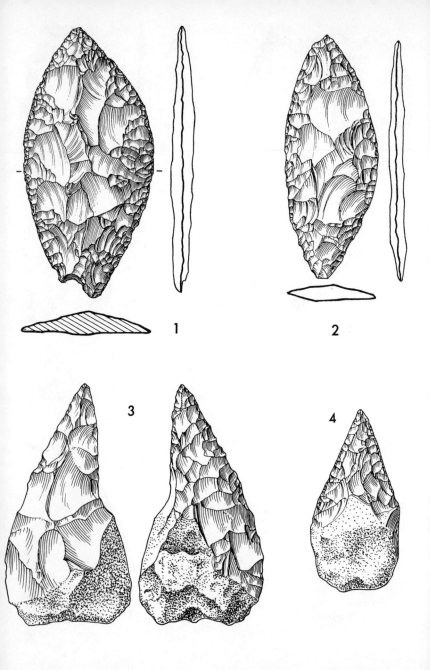

1

2

3

4

*Figure 38* 1,2, two 'Blattspitzen' from Mauern
Cave. The general outline can be compared
to that of Solutrean laurel leaves, but
the technique of fabrication is quite different.
3,4, Micoquian handaxes from Bockstein (Germany).

tradition type A, at Spy. The site at Godarville (excavated by
J. de Heinzelin, but results so far unpublished) belongs also to
the Mousterian of Acheulean tradition. At Clypot near Soignies,
the same researcher found some typical Mousterian. Denticulate
Mousterian has not so far been discovered.

In Switzerland, Mousterian is rare and belongs to the 'alpine'
type. Certain sites are said to have produced large quantities of
bone-splinters that have been utilised; but these are perhaps the
product of natural actions, imitating wear on the edges.

In Germany, Mousterian of Acheulean tradition is known by
surface discoveries of fine triangular and cordiform handaxes near
Ziegenhein near Treysa (the research work was undertaken by
A. Luttropp). The site probably also contains some Quina-type
Mousterian. Deposits in the loess at Wallertheim near Mainz may
also belong to the Acheulean-tradition Mousterian. At Lebenstedt
near Brunswick it is rather a question of a belated Acheulean. The
most interesting type is the Mousterian containing foliated tools
(*Blattspitzen*; see figure 38,1,2). It is found in various sites, for
example at Mauern near Neuburg. According to Gisela Freund, it
would probably be derived from a Klause-type Micoquian.
According to Zotz, four levels are shown at Mauern, grouped into
two stages, the second belonging to Würm III and so to the Upper
Palaeolithic age. This upper stage II produces flakes that are more or
less Levallois in type, numerous scrapers of various types, no
genuine Mousterian points, and more than half are foliated implements, reminiscent in outline but not in flaking technique of the
Solutrean laurel-leaves. Stage I, which is older, possesses some
Mousterian points, some scrapers, only a few small handaxes, and
foliated tools of rougher quality than in the upper level.

The German Micoquian occurs in several Würmian deposits, at
Bockstein in the Lonetal (figure 38, 3,4) and at Klause near Neu
Essing in Bavaria. Alongside the Micoquian-style handaxes there

*Figure 39* Mousterian from
Tata (Hungary). 1, striated pebble;
2, amulet made from a nummulite
and engraved with a cross; 3, bone
retoucher; 4, mammoth ivory 'churinga'.

are flat foliated handaxes cut out of thin flint slabs (there may have
been some foliated forms at La Micoque) and some backed handaxes with triangular cross-section, not absolutely unknown at La
Micoque or in the Combe-Grenal Upper Acheulean. Probably
there are links between the La Micoque Micoquian and the type
found in Germany, but the latter presents a somewhat different
facies.

In Central Europe the Mousterian exists in a variety of types. In
Czechoslovakia it is difficult to say to what type it belongs, although there is one broken triangular handaxe at Kulna (Moravia).
At Sipka and at Certova-Dira (also in Moravia) there have been
finds of the Mousterian, and at the former a Neanderthal child's
maxillary bone has been found. In Slovakia there are various
known sites, mostly open-air.

In Hungary the Subalyuk cave in the Bükk Mountains has yielded
a western-looking Mousterian which is probably typical. The
Büdopest cave, also in the Bükk Mountains, has produced an industry which, following Vértes, comprises seven per cent Mousterian
points, forty-nine per cent scrapers, some limaces, and two or three
*Blattspitzen*. There is an important site at Tata, sixty kilometres
west of Budapest, dated by the radiocarbon method at about
50,000 years, which would make it Middle Mousterian. The very
plentiful industry belongs to one particular type. It is generally
flaked from pebbles, its dimensions are small, and there is not
much of the Levallois technique. There is a high percentage of
scrapers, and at first sight one would take this to be a rather special
Quina-type Mousterian. But the genuine Quina scrapers are few
and far between, and there are a very large number of scrapers with
bifacial retouch which are also mostly not of the Quina type. We
should note a mammoth-ivory 'churinga', which was once covered
with ochre, and an amulet made from nummulite engraved with a
cross (see figure 39).

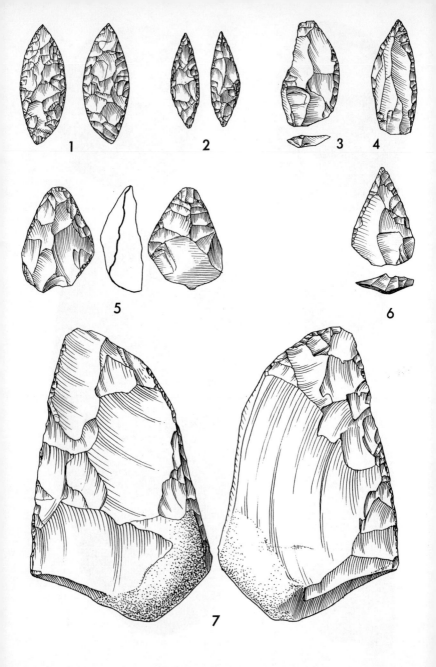

*Figure 40* Mousterian from Kokkinopilos (Greece). 113
1,2, foliate bifacial points; 3, convex side-scraper;
4,6, Mousterian points; 5, broken tip
of a handaxe.—Wylotne (Poland);
7, 'Prodnik', a special type of handaxe.


In Austria in the Teufelslucken cave there is some Mousterian
with at least one handaxe and in the cave at Repolust implements
which, according to the description given, perhaps represent
denticulate Mousterian unless it is a question of battered specimens.
There are various Mousterian assemblages in Rumania, one of
them with handaxes, points and scrapers at La Izvor near Ripiceni,
probably more akin to the Rissian Mousterian than to the Mousterian of Acheulean tradition. In the Dobrudja there is some perhaps
typical Mousterian. From what has been published, it is difficult to
tell to what type the finds in Bulgaria belong. A site to be noted in
Yugoslavia is Krapina, Croatia, which has yielded numerous
Neanderthal human remains of a rather special kind. The existence
of Merck's rhinoceros among the fauna had suggested the Riss/
Würm interglacial period, but they may indeed be Würmian, for
(especially in this region) this animal is not an absolute indication of
the interglacial period.

Mousterian deposits have recently been found in Greece, and
even a Neanderthal skull. This skull – which has no archaeological
context – comes from Petralona, not far from Thessalonika. At
Kokkinopilos (figure 40, 1 to 6) in Epiros, Dekaris, Higgs and Hay
found in silt deposits a fairly rich Mousterian, with Levallois flakes
and points, Mousterian points, scrapers, some end-scrapers and
burins, four bifacial foliate points and a broken handaxe. But apart
from the handaxe and the foliate points, this industry would be
fairly like a typical Mousterian. There is also some Mousterian in
the Peloponesus (research by A. Leroi-Gourhan).

In Poland there is a variety of Middle Palaeolithic material. The
rock-shelter at Wylotne, twenty-two kilometres to the north of
Cracow, has produced several layers dating from Würm I and
Würm I/II (French classification). The bottom layer has produced a
prolonged Acheulean or Micoquian with handaxes, lanceolate or
sub-triangular, *prodniks* (figure 40, 7) a kind of bifacial knife

*Figure 41* Micoquian from La Micoque (layer 6). Row 1, from left to right: four handaxes, three scrapers. Row 2: four handaxes, two scrapers, one point. Row 3: three handaxes, two broken foliates (?), two scrapers.

115

*Figure 42* Kiik-Koba. 1, handaxe, Starocelie;
2, 6, foliate tools; 3, 7 canted scraper;
4, Mousterian point; 5, convex side-scraper.

reminiscent of the backed bifacial tools in the Micoquian, but slightly different, scrapers, etc. The upper level has yielded an industry showing clearcut derivation from the former but with fewer handaxes and more *prodniks*. An analogous and more or less contemporary industry has been found in the Okiennik cave and in the Ciemma cave, where layer 6 contains *prodniks* but no true handaxes. In Würm II, there are perhaps some traces of Mousterian of Acheulean tradition in the Nietoperzowa cave.

In the European USSR, Mousterian is well represented. The deposit at Kiik Koba in the Crimea, twenty-five kilometres east of Simferopol, has often been attributed – as far as the upper layer is concerned – to the Micoquian, to which it does in fact show some resemblances. But it is nearer to the German or Polish Micoquian than to that of La Micoque, with its lanceolate bifacial pieces with triangular-section (figure 42, 1) and nearer still to the undoubted Mousterian at Starocelie, also in the Crimea, where there are likewise some foliated bifacial forms. This latter industry (figure 42, 2 to 5) is considered by Soviet archaeologists to be Upper Mousterian, Kiik Koba belonging to the Lower Mousterian.

At Volgograd (formerly Stalingrad), on the right bank of the Volga, is the site of Sukhaya Metcheka. The layer runs at a depth of twenty metres and has been excavated over an area of 600 square metres, yielding a Mousterian industry with small atypical handaxes and others reminiscent of certain pieces at Starocelie, which are in turn reminiscent of the Polish *prodniks*; some flat lanceolate handaxes, some subcordiform handaxes, points, end-scrapers, various scrapers, foliated pieces, etc. This special-type Mousterian (see figure 43) might well be connected with that at Starocelie.

But the most impressive discovery was made at Molodova I, on the banks of the Dniester, in western Ukraine. In the lower layer, which would date from the Upper Mousterian, Tchernych discovered the remains of a hut: an oval ring measuring seven by ten

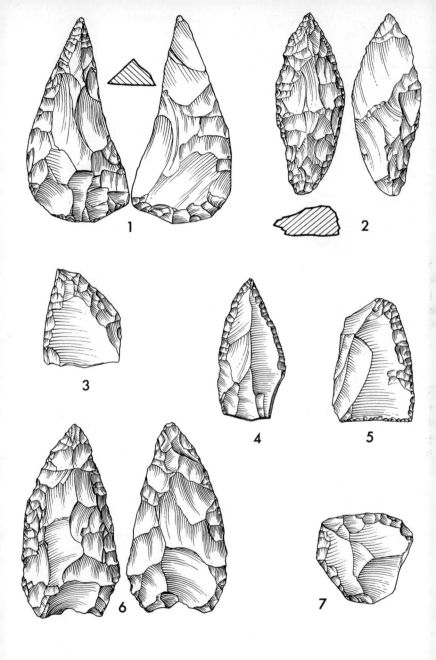

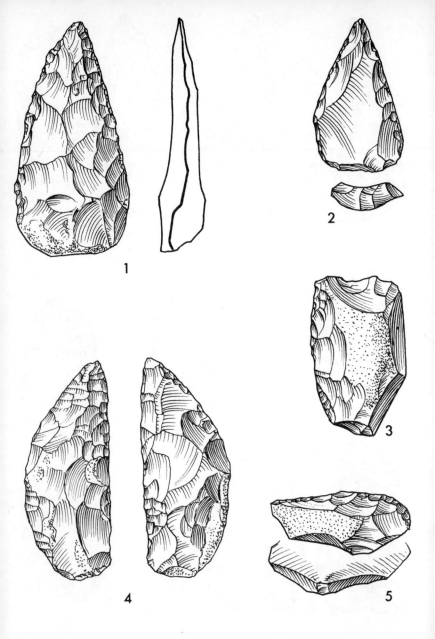

*Figure 43* Mousterian of
Volgograd (Russia). 1, handaxe;
2, Mousterian point; 3, side-scraper;
4, bifacial tool recalling the Polish
'prodniks'; 5, transversal scraper.

metres composed of mammoth bones, twelve broken skulls,
thirty-four shoulder-blades and pelvises, fifty-one limb-bones,
fourteen tusks and five jaws. Inside were fifteen small hearths
(see figure 51). The industry, which includes points, scrapers and
discoid or Levallois cores, is somewhat reminiscent of the typical
Western Mousterian.

There is an abundance of Mousterian in Italy in various forms.
Quite close to the French frontier, at Grimaldi, in the Grotte du
Prince which was excavated from 1895 to 1901, the three lower
hearths were Ferrassie-type Mousterian, certainly Würmian
although containing Merck's rhinoceros and even, in the lowest
hearth, some hippopotamus remains. In Venetia there is certainly
some typical Mousterian, and some of the Quina type, and even
perhaps some Denticulate Mousterian. In the Roman region there
is the Pontinian, found in open-air deposits as well as in caves (such
as the Guattari cave at Mort-Circé, where a Neanderthal skull was
discovered on the ground). It is a Quina-type Mousterian, the
original characteristic being that it is flaked from small pebbles.
Because of its small size, certain authors have wanted to call it
Micromousterian; but it is difficult to see how palaeolithic men
could have obtained large tools from small pebbles! It is also found
beneath the Upper Palaeolithic in the Fossellone cave, where it may
be interstratified with Denticulate Mousterian. The fauna is of the
'warm' type, although the industries are certainly Würmian. There
are no certain traces of Mousterian of Acheulean tradition in Italy.

Mousterian is equally common in Spain. In the Cantabrian
region at Castillo the older and perhaps Acheulean levels are overlaid by several Mousterian layers. The lower layer is of Quina-type
Mousterian, richer than usual in denticulates, which – like the
Pontinian – is rather special in appearance because it is flaked from
small pebbles. The upper layer is rather different, with Levallois
technique more prominent, there being fewer scrapers and more

plentiful denticulates. Above all, there are some handaxes and a good many flake-cleavers made out of large ophite flakes. Here the Mousterian clearly shows the continuing influence of Africa as in the Spanish Acheulean. This special type, which we have proposed to call Vasconian, spills over into south-western France, as we saw above.

On the other side of Spain the province of Alicante has yielded what is probably typical Mousterian. The same is true for Cariguela cave, near Piñar, north of Grenada, where there is a magnificent typical Mousterian recalling both the North African and the Dordogne types. This deposit has produced human remains, as have the sites at Gibraltar.

In Catalonia the Romani Shelter explored by E. Ripoll Perello has produced a Mousterian which De Lumley connects with the Denticulate Mousterian.

Mousterian has also been found in Portugal.

# 9 The Mousterian stage in Africa

At this period, Africa falls into two distinct zones, a northern one – more or less linked with Europe and the Middle East, containing Mousterian in the strict sense, and a zone to the south of the Sahara, containing only Mousteroid industries more or less approximating to the true Mousterian.

There is a genuine Mousterian industry in North Africa, although its existence has sometimes been denied because of some tanged points in certain of its layers which caused them to be called Aterian. But as Professor Balout observes, it is as yet rare and imperfectly studied. In Morocco the only certain deposit is at Djebel Irhoud, a recent discovery which would appear – pending a full inventory – to be a typical Mousterian. Human remains of Neanderthal man have been found at this site. For the present, Mousterian is about equally scarce in Algeria. There is some mediocre quality Mousterian at Cape Tenes, in the Lighthouse cave. Another and more certain site is at Retaïmia, in the Chelif valley in Oran. What has so far been published, and Tixier's observations upon it, would suggest that there were in fact several industries represented, one of which was reminiscent of Quina-type Mousterian. In Tunisia there are definitely five Mousterian deposits: Wadi Akarit north of Gabes, El Guettar near Gafsa, Aïn Meterchem (tufas) north-west of Djebel Chambi near the Algerian frontier, Sidi-Zin in the tufas overlying the Acheulean, and Aïn Mhrotta, near Kairouan. At Aïn Meterchem, as at El Guettar, there is a fine Mousterian assemblage which by its richness in scrapers and its Levallois technique has been taken as probably akin to the Ferrassie-type Mousterian but which would no doubt more likely correspond to a North African facies of typical Mousterian. These two series (there are several layers at El Guettar, excavated by Dr Gruet) each contain one tanged artifact of Aterian type.

Following on from the Mousterian, and probably extending over the European Upper Palaeolithic period, there is a typically North-

African industry: the Aterian, considered nowadays to be the equivalent of the European Upper Palaeolithic and which we shall therefore be looking at later.

In Cyrenaica, McBurney's excavations have uncovered a Mousterian assemblage in the Haua Fteah cave, dated about $44,300 \pm 3,000$ years before our era, and in the tufas of Hajj Creiem, in the Wadi Derna. This last one seems to belong to the typical Mousterian. The Mousterian is also known in Egypt (under the name of Levalloisian or Levalloiso-Mousterian), in the Kharga oasis. The 'Khargian' on the other hand is probably only the result of small Mousterian flakes having been crushed under foot, e.g. by animals coming to drink.

Near Wadi Halfa in Nubia, Guichard has recently described various Mousterian or Mousteroid industries having no tanged artifacts, but still sometimes containing handaxes, and forms closely akin to Sangoan picks. Sometimes finer foliated points occur, recalling those of the final Aterian, Stillbayan or evolved Sangoan periods.

South of the Sahara, the 'Middle Stone Age' corresponds more or less to the Mousterian stage from the typological point of view, but chronologically it is partly contemporary with the European Upper Palaeolithic. In the more humid conditions of the Gamblian (last pluvial) phase, man begins to occupy regions that were formerly uninhabited. This is a period of diversification, with numerous local facies covering more or less vast areas. Their chronology is as yet imperfectly defined. We shall be studying them along with the Upper Palaeolithic.

The industries classed as belonging to what is sometimes called 'the First intermediate' are clearly of the Mousterian stage. There are two main ones, the Fauresmith and the Sangoan, which seem to correspond to different habitats and environments, the Sangoan being a forest industry, the Fauresmith belonging to more open and

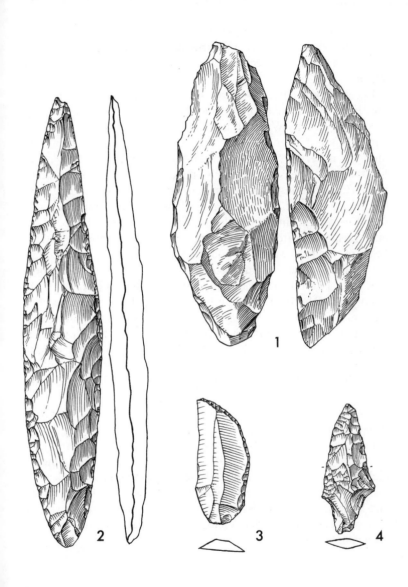

*Figure 44* Middle Palaeolithic tools from Africa. 1, Sangoan pick from Sangoa; 2, bifacial point, Lower Lupembian of Angola; 3, Lupembian backed knife, Angola; 4, tanged point, Upper Lupembian of Angola.

steppe-like country. These industries date from the beginning of the Gamblian, or a little earlier, and so are contemporary with the Würm.

In central and eastern Africa – which are more densely forested – the 'First intermediate' culture is represented by the Sangoan. It was discovered by Wayland in 1920, the type-site being the hills at Sango Bay in Uganda on the western shore of Lake Victoria. This industry is certainly derived from the Acheulean, preserving its handaxes – at least in its early stages – although with smaller proportions and less well made. New features are some large picks (see figure 44) and a kind of large plane, which was indeed to be found in certain final Acheulean assemblages. This change in the implements has often been attributed to forest adaptation and the need for intensive work in wood. In Angola and the Lower Congo, the Sangoan starts with an assemblage very like that of the Uganda-type zone, but it then develops in a different way. At Kalambo Falls in northern Rhodesia Sangoan has been dated by the radiocarbon method at about 40,000 years ago; it is thus contemporary with European Upper Mousterian. It is followed by the Lupemban.

In southern Rhodesia there is Bambezian, which would seem to be a kind of Sangoan, with discoid cores, points, scrapers, denticulates, thick end-scrapers or planes, some oval handaxes and some picks.

An evolved Sangoan is to be found in isolation at Primrose Ridge, near Johannesburg.

In Uganda the site of Nsengesi in the Kagera valley has produced, as well as the Sangoan type, an early Sangoan on a thirty-metre-high terrace; it is a little more evolved than the final Acheulean. It contains handaxes, cleavers, picks, large 'knives' on lateral flakes, and large scrapers. The Sangoan occurs everywhere in the western part of Kenya, near Lake Victoria. In Tanzania there have only been isolated finds.

In South Africa, the Fauresmith (so called after Fauresmith of the Orange Free State) is a kind of Mousterian of Acheulean tradition with classical Levalloisian technique, including Levalloisian triangular points. The handaxes – which are smaller than in the Acheulean – are elongated cordiforms or cordiforms of standard type, sometimes with scaly retouch. There are still cleavers but they are smaller, and numerous flake tools, the percentage increasing as the industry evolves, whilst the handaxes become rarer. The Saldanha skull was probably associated with this industry.

In East Africa – according to Sonia Cole – there are Fauresmith types in the highlands of Kenya and Ethiopia; but they seem to be confined to high altitudes, and their zone is not coextensive with that of the Sangoan except on the north-eastern shore of Lake Victoria. Kenya Fauresmith was first of all called Nanyukian; and there too it would seem to belong to the dry period before the Gamblian, its typical tools including small handaxes and cleavers, numerous stone balls and flake-tools. The most northerly point, a surface site about twenty-five kilometres south of Gondar, was discovered by D. Clark in Ethiopia during World War Two.

There exists in the 'horn' of Africa, in former British Somaliland, some Acheulean-Levalloisian, that is to say, Acheulean with Levallois flakes, often classified as 'First intermediate'. At Obok in French Somaliland there are some poor handaxes, no cleavers, and more Levallois flakes. This is perhaps a kind of transition to the 'Lower Levalloisian' found in the north-west of Somaliland, an industry with Levallois flakes but only very occasional scrapers and points. The 'Upper Levalloisian' which is certainly late, is smaller and now and again presents a bifacial retouch that foreshadows the Stillbay culture.

# 10 The Mousterian stage in Asia

In the Middle East, as in North Africa, the Mousterian is much closer to the European Mousterian than to the African industries. This Mousterian complex is known from numerous caves and shelters. In Syria the bottom of the deposits at Jabrud has produced, as well as Acheulean, a rather special industry known as Jabrudian, a kind of Quina-type Mousterian in which there are a few transverse scrapers but a great many canted ones. There are various Mousterian layers above this, generally with definite Levallois features. Layer 12 is probably a local Mousterian of Acheulean tradition, layer 9 a denticulated Mousterian, layers 10 and 8 a Mousterian in which there are still some handaxes, and layer 7 a typical Mousterian, etc. Layer 5 is worth dwelling on more fully. It has produced Rust's Micromousterian, and the average dimensions of the implements are in fact small. Here, this is not because the raw material consisted of small pebbles – as at Mont-Circó and Castillo – for there are abundant large flint nodules round about Jabrud. This small size must be intentional. This Micromousterian assemblage seems to be of the denticulated Mousterian type. Layers 4 to 2 are typical Mousterian. In a general way, what separates these industries from Western Mousterian is a greater use of blades and the larger part played by gravers, especially after the pre-Aurignacian level (Layer 15).

This Levallois-technique Mousterian seems to be rather late, belonging certainly to Würm II and probably even continuing into the interstadial II/III.

In the Lebanon, there is Mousterian material at the bottom of the very fine site at Ksar'Akil. Other deposits have also yielded various kinds of Mousterian.

In the Mount Carmel district of Israel Mousterian is found above Acheulean at Et-Tabun, and also at Es Skhül. Unfortunately the excavations took place some thirty years ago, and all the layers were not thoroughly distinguished. Taken as a whole, this

*Figure 45* Geographical position of some
Palaeolithic sites in the Middle East. 1, Belbasi;
2, Beldibi; 3, Ksar Akil; 4, Yabrud; 5, Banat Yaqoub;
6, Djebel Kafzeh; 7, Ubeidiya; 8, Tabun; 9–12, Umm Qatafa,
Abu Sif, Et Tabban, Sahba; 13, Shanidar; 14, Pelagrawa; 15, Zarzi.

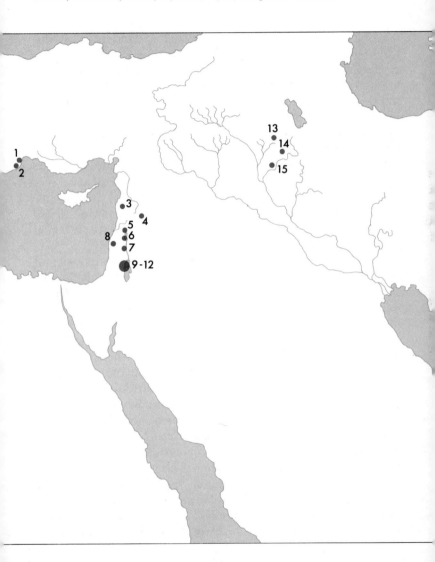

must be typical Mousterian similar to that at Jabrud; and in this Mousterian deposit human remains have been found, morphologically intermediate between Neanderthal and modern man; but it has not been possible for the moment to decide whether this is a transitional form or a cross-breed. In the desert of Judea in Jordan, the Abu-Sif cave contains final Acheulean at its base, surmounted by a marked Levallois and blade-rich Mousterian, with long slender points, scrapers sometimes on blades, and infrequent gravers. The absence of handaxes and the abundance of points would class it as typical Mousterian, similar to layer 10 at Jabrud. The neighbouring Sahba cave has yielded similar implements. Tabban, not far away, has produced a rather different Mousterian, with fewer blades though still Levallois. The same is true of Umm Naqus (excavations by R. Neuville).

There is also some Mousterian in Turkey. In the Kurd region of Iraq, the fine site of Shanidar has been excavated by R. Solecki. There are several metres of Mousterian below Neolithic and Upper Palaeolithic levels, which have not yet been described in detail. This Mousterian has produced several classical Neanderthal skeletons. In Kurdistan, too, the earlier excavations of D. Garrod at Hazar Merd had yielded a Mousterian similar to that at Abu Sif.

In the Asiatic part of the southern USSR, south of the Caucasus, there are several Mousterian deposits, particularly at the Akhchtyrskaya cave in the Sochi region, which has produced a Mousterian assemblage with at least one foliated piece, some points, some scrapers, and perhaps some rough handaxes. There is also Mousterian overlying the Acheulean in the Koudaro cave. On the east coast of the Caspian sea, the Mousterian has been noted at five surface sites. In Central Asia, in the Baisun region of Uzbekistan, the Teshik-Tash cave has been attributed by Soviet writers to the Mindel/Riss interglacial, but might equally well belong to a Würmian-interstadial or to the early Würm. It was excavated in

1938–9 by Okladnikov, and produced five archaeological layers and a Neanderthal child's burial surrounded by a circle of wild goat horns. The site was relatively poor in implements, and the industry hardly seems to have shown any variation from one layer to another. It contains rough handaxes, choppers, a few blades and Levallois flakes, lateral or transverse scrapers, either single or double, etc. Taken as a whole, this Mousterian is vaguely reminiscent of the Quina type by virtue of its retouching, but belongs no doubt to a special type. Seventy-five kilometres from Tashkent, the cave at Khodzhikenskaya has recently (1958) produced similar industrial finds.

Forty-five kilometres south of Samarkand, the Aman Kutan cave has yielded a dozen implements, some traces of fire, and a Neanderthal-type human femur. This industry has been attributed to the Tayacian and to the end of the Mindel/Riss, but its fauna is similar to that at Teshik-Tash and it might well be Mousterian made from poor raw material. In the Syr-Daria valley, near Leninabad, there are some surface sites which have been ascribed to the Mousterian.

In northern India, the upper Soan could well be an industry belonging to the Mousterian stage, although it has been dated – without any absolute evidence – as belonging to the Riss.

The Mousterian in the broad sense has been discovered at several places in China, though there is no complete certainty about its chronological position. The site that appears the most important at present is at Shui-tung-kou, in the Ordos region, quite close to the Great Wall. There in the loess Teilhard discovered several hearths at different levels yielding – according to his account – an absolutely homogeneous industry. The chief hearth contained a rich industry, which was studied by Breuil, who diagnosed it as a culture 'seemingly half way between a very evolved Mousterian and a nascent Aurignacian, or a combination of these two!' We have had occasion to restudy this industry, which is kept in Paris at the Institut de Paléontologie Humaine. Sure enough it is a Levallois-technique Mousterian, with blades well represented (thirty-one per cent of blades or blade tools), with twenty-seven per cent scrapers, 16·6 per cent denticulates, twenty-eight per cent implements of Upper Palaeolithic type (end-scrapers, burins, borers, occasional backed knives, flakes and truncated blades), a few poor handaxes (about one per cent, contrary to what Breuil had supposed), and about two per cent of choppers. In addition, there were discs, bladelets, and some splintered pieces.

The impression given is in fact that of a very evolved Mousterian in the process of transition to an Upper Palaeolithic stage, but of a type which, taken all round, has not much connection with Western forms, though it might well be a precursor to the Siberian-type Upper Palaeolithic. It is interesting to note the presence in one of the hearths of a fairly fine unifacial point. At the present moment it is difficult to say whether this industry is contemporary with western Eurasiatic Mousterian, or whether it belongs to the Upper Palaeolithic period and so to the late subdivision of the Stone Age.

# 11 A general review of the Old and Middle Palaeolithic

We have now reached a point – namely, the end of the second Würmian stage in Europe – where it would perhaps be as well to look back over the course we have travelled. Modern man – that is, we ourselves – is about to appear on the scene, and has perhaps even made his appearance already at some point on the earth. Man now occupies all the ancient world, but has not yet penetrated into the American and Australian continents, not to mention the cluster of Polynesian islands which will not be reached till well after the Palaeolithic Age (see figure 46).

As we set out from the very lowest levels we see two or three zones dating from the Upper Villafranchian, or rather, for the moment, one zone and two find-spots – Africa from the Cape to the Maghreb on the one hand, and Le Vallonet on the south coast of France and perhaps Rumania on the other. In southern Africa the Australopithecines have left numerous remains, but no absolute proof that they were true men and tool-makers. In eastern Africa other and perhaps more evolved australopithecines (*Homo habilis*) were certainly tool-makers.

In the Maghreb and at Le Vallonet there are not for the moment any finds of human remains, but there are implements. It is impossible for the present to say whether Le Vallonet is exactly contemporary with Olduvai, or later. It is tempting to see East Africa as the centre in which man originated; but after all, if Europe has only one scanty cave to set against a gorge so rich in fossils, this may be due to its periglacial position which has resulted in the scouring of a number of caves, thus emptying them of their ancient contents or it may be due to the early date at which most of the excavations in the fossil-bearing sites took place – sites which may have contained Villafranchian implements that would at that period certainly have gone unrecognised. As for the human remains, the Leakeys' experience, in common with that of all palaeontologists, shows that their great find resulted from a combination of patience and luck. However this may be, there was certainly a population of as yet very primitive people alive in the Villafranchian period, though in becoming tool-makers they had taken the great step that would henceforward divide them from the animals.

Can we form any picture of the way they lived? Their manner of life appears to have been different in south Africa from what it was in the north or in the east, and this difference may perhaps be significant. In southern Africa they lived in caves or fissures, or at any rate made use of them, in a countryside that was probably not very different then from what it is now. They were no doubt hunters, or took advantage of the hunting-remains of the wild animals; and if the dented skulls of the baboons are really due to them, we must imagine them hunting in troops, for baboons live in bands and are dangerous. Australopithecines cannot have been much more than 1·40 mm (4 ft 6 in) in height, and would have been no match for a baboon in single combat even with the very rudimentary weapon of a chipped pebble-tool. As for Paranthropus, he was taller, heavier and more powerful, and probably a vegetarian. In eastern Africa the Australopithecines lived on the shore of lakes, were certainly tool-makers, and hunted small animals or the young of larger species. It is possible too that they hunted Paranthropus, and that the *Zinjanthropus* find in the habitat strewn with implements does not represent their maker, but the remains of a meal.

Very early on, perhaps at the same time as at Olduvai, there is evidence in Europe and probably in Asia of the existence of australopithecines. The expansion of the human race has begun, an expansion destined to cause man – alone among the mammals – to occupy a whole planet, from the polar regions to the equator. Through lack of a sufficiently accurate chronology, the direction of this expansion is not as yet absolutely clear. But one thing is certain: from this stage onwards, man has been an adaptable animal whose progress has been barred neither by differences of climate nor of environment. And yet his hold upon the external world was as yet remarkably feeble. He was but a moderately skilful hunter possessing only very rudimentary tools, and had not yet discovered fire. But although in the Paranthropus form he was destined to share the fate of other species who failed to adapt themselves, as Australopithecus the future belonged to him. His brain was developing, he was increasing in stature, and soon he had reached the stage of Pithecanthropus. But this evolution was very slow, and lasted perhaps 600,000 years. At the Pithecanthropus level, it would seem that the division between the two principal Lower Palaeolithic industries had already come about. Certain of these Pithecanthropines made handaxes in Africa, in Europe and perhaps in Asia, whilst others remained faithful to the ancient forms such as those of the Choukoutien or Vertesszöllös.

Pithecanthropus, like his *Australopithecus* ancestors, lived either in the open air, on the banks of rivers or lakes, or in caves. And now he had taken a decisive step forward and was in possession of fire, at any rate in certain places. He used it intensively at Choukoutien, and there are traces of it at Vertesszöllös. In Africa there would be no evidence of fire until much later, perhaps because the climate made it less necessary, or because the traces of it have survived less well in strongly oxydising conditions. Armed with fire, which he knew how to keep alive but perhaps could not yet produce, man was able to make his way into the big caves and occupy them for long periods in spite of wild beasts. We have very little idea of the numerical strength of these human groups, but it cannot have been very great – perhaps ten or a dozen. Man was now hunting large-sized game and his implements were better assorted. As well as choppers and handaxes, he began to have specialised scrapers, knives and borers. But at this distant Mindelian period – perhaps some 500,000 years ago – man was still a rarity upon earth, just a few groups scattered here and there over the vast spaces of the planet.

During the period corresponding to the interglacial Mindel/Riss, progress continued, physically as well as culturally. In Africa and in Europe this was the time of transition from the Abbevillian to the Acheulean, or (for the non-handaxe line) to the Clactonian. But from the fact that the Abbevillian – and probably the lower Acheulean – are the work of Pithecanthropus, it does not necessarily follow that the whole of the Acheulean, right up to its end, was also his work. At that period, Europe and the whole temperate zone seems to have been covered by massive forests, giving an environment which had ceased to be favourable to man when the ancestors of the australopithecines turned their back on it for ever and advanced into the savannahs. But there must also have been large zones of prairie or savannah there as well. In Africa, the variations in vegetation must have been less marked.

It is at this level that we encounter the problem of convergences, or of belated evolutions. It seems certain that handaxes developed from chopping-tools (Oldowan) by a process of extending the chipped-face first of all to the greater part of the pebble, then to its complete circumference. This development took place very early in Africa (by the middle of the Olduvai layer ii), and can be likewise traced near Casablanca. In Europe we do not at present possess the transition stage between the Vallonet pebble tools and the Abbevillian, but this evolution must have taken place in the interglacial Günz/Mindel period and the implements must have suffered the fate of most of the interglacial industries. It seems difficult to believe that there was one single evolutionary centre (Olduvai for example) from which the influences of more evolved peoples radiated at various epochs. Just as there is the problem of knowing whether the invention of the tool took place before or after the australopithecan diaspora, so is it a matter of speculation whether the evolution from the pebble tool to the handaxe took place at various places in the earth, starting out from one common stage.

| | Europe | | Africa | | India | Asia S.E | S.W |
|---|---|---|---|---|---|---|---|
| 10,000 Würm III and IV | Upper Palaeolithic | | Capsian Ibero-Maurusian Aterian | Egyptian up.pal. Dabban, etc. Lupembian | (?) | | Upper Palaeolithic |
| Würm I and II 80,000 | Mousterian Final Acheulean | | Mousterian Upper Acheulean | Sangoan | Late Soan | Final Anyathian | Mousterian Final Acheulean |
| Riss/ Würm 200,000 | Upper Acheulean | Pre-Mousterian | Upper Acheulean | | Upper Acheulean Upper Soan | Fenho Complex Anyathian | Acheulean |
| Riss | Upper Acheulean Middle Acheulean | 'Tayacian' Clactonian | Acheulean | | Acheulean Soan | Choukoutien loc. 15 | Acheulean |
| Mindel/ Riss | Middle Acheulean Early Acheulean | Clactonian | Acheulean | | Soan? | (NEW ANYATHIAN) | Old Acheulean |
| Mindel 500,000? | Early Acheulean Abbevillian | Clactonian | 'Old Acheulean' | | Acheulean? Old Soan? | Choukoutien loc. 1 Choukoutien loc. 13 (OLD ANYATHIAN) | Ubeidyia |
| Günz/ Mindel | Flakes? | | Oldowan | | | | |
| Günz | ? | | Oldowan | | | | |
| Danube 1·9 million Biber | UPPER VILLAFRANCHIAN | Vallonet pebble tools Gamblian: Late Würm | Olduvai I.1 (Oldowan) | | | | |

An interesting case is that of the Padjitanian, an industry containing typical handaxes, but in an isolated cul-de-sac in Java without any known links at present (except perhaps Tampanian) with the nearest handaxe zone in India. Is this a case of retarded evolution on the part of a people belonging to the chopper-chopping-tool group, who rather late in the day invented the bifacial implement independently, and for reasons unknown?

What meaning is to be ascribed to this separation between a handaxe and a non-handaxe line? Why was this implement so much appreciated by some, and unknown to or rejected by others? It might well be thought – and this is an often expressed point of view – that this is only a matter of different aspects of one and the same culture, corresponding to different activities. But how then are we to explain the fact that over by far the greatest part of Asia, and even of eastern Europe, there are no handaxes at all? (see figure 47). This cannot be due to environment, since both types were going to prosper in the most varied surroundings from periglacial to subtropical, and would seem to have ensured the survival of their makers as successfully in the one case as in the other. And what special activities could there have been in Europe and Africa which were unknown in Asia? Raw material does not enter into it, for there are handaxes of limestone, of quartz, of various volcanic rocks, and even of granite. It would certainly look as though we are dealing with two different cultural lines; and this is no doubt a first sign of that cultural inertia by reason of which man does not change his way of life except under the threat of the worst possible conditions or the impetus of exceptional events or individuals.

When the Rissian ice age brought back cold or humid conditions, the Pithecanthropines were no more than a memory. Remains such as those at Steinheim, Swanscombe and La Chaise show us that man was now at the pre-Neanderthal stage, and that his brain capacity was larger. Tools began really to become standardised, although they continued to evolve. There can be no doubt that the men of this time had a perfectly clear mental image of the object to be made before they set about making it. The flaking techniques were now becoming more refined. In addition to the stone striker, which was still in use, man had discovered that finer work could be done and a straighter and sharper edge produced by working the stone with a striker of softer material than the stone itself. This was a discovery of the first importance, which would later make possible works of art like the Solutrean laurel leaves.

Nor can there be any doubt that man was acquainted with simple geometrical forms derived from the triangle, the ellipse or the oval, for he reproduced them by the thousand in his most carefully-worked handaxes. This perfect regularity adds little to the object by way of efficiency as a tool, and we should perhaps see in it the first tentative expression of the aesthetic sense. This (or perhaps slightly earlier) was also the period when the Levallois technique was invented, presupposing not only a conception of the tool's final form but also the various successive stages required and the difficulties to be encountered. We have numerous Levallois cores that have been cast aside before the detachment of the flake because of some unforeseeable defect in the flint which made this detachment impossible. On some of them, an attempt has been made all the same; for optimists have always existed!

This Levallois technique also poses another problem, for it seems to have been invented at various times and in various places, and in a variety of ways. In South Africa, it still seems to have been preceded by the lateral Levallois technique, the so-called 'Victoria-West', seemingly unknown in Europe, in which the technique begins with fairly atypical and clumsy cores – in the Cagny Acheulean, for example – with nothing of the Victoria-West about them. The Levallois technique also appears in the Clactonian line; in Europe, this might perhaps indicate a borrowing from the

138

Acheulean. Yet there are Levallois flakes in the extreme East.

An interesting point, recalling what happened with the handaxes, is that this Levallois technique has had its ups and downs. From the middle of the Riss, Acheuleans in the north of France used it enthusiastically; but certain tribes or groups seem only reluctantly to have used it. This presents us with a second dichotomy: between the groups where this technique was favoured and those where it was almost non-existent. And here it is not simply a question of culture, period or raw material. The Acheulean-tradition Mousterians of Le Pech de l'Azé, for instance, hardly used this method at all although they knew of it, whilst those of Le Moustier, clearly their contemporaries and not having any superior raw material, used it a great deal. Technique apart, these two groups are practically identical. And other groups produced Levallois flakes from the most unpromising material.

From the end of the Rissian, the Acheulean implements become highly diversified, and although there will still be some changes in the type of handaxes or the style of the flake tools, the latter are now of well-established types, to which the Mousterians will only add variations. Even tools often considered to be the invention of the Upper Palaeolithic were Acheulean creations – such as gravers, scrapers on the ends of flakes or blades, borers, truncated blades and flakes, and backed knives. But they still play only a minor part.

As well as stone, man certainly used wood, although there is but scanty proof of this. He also no doubt began to realise that bone is a material that may be worked with the appropriate techniques; but here too we have little documentation. He was a regular hunter of large game (the bison, horse and stag), and could even attack the giants (the hippopotamus, rhinoceros and elephant). It seems certain that he could only get the better of them by cunning, for a wooden spear or even a flint point (which are rarely found as yet) would hardly pierce the skin of a pachyderm. And so those animals

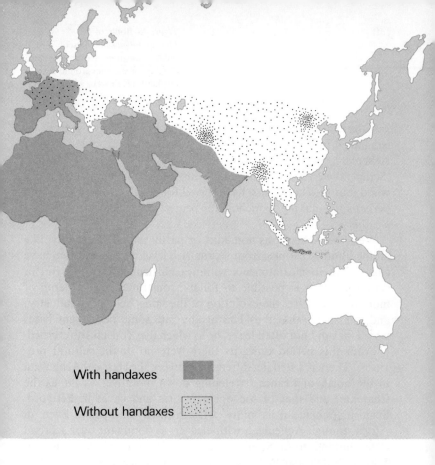

With handaxes

Without handaxes

were probably caught in traps, either artificial (pits) or natural ones such as marshes, into which the animals were driven by frightening them with shouting, by feigning a concerted attack, or by setting fire to the grasses. It was most probably in this way that the Acheuleans of Torralba-Ambrona killed their elephants when they were half engulfed in mud, and that a primitive Archimedes had the idea of using their tusks as levers for shifting their enormous bulk and making it easier to cut them up (see figure 48). It would appear difficult to imagine all this without a language in which to express actions and the notion of sequence in time.

Although we have the example of the Fuegians living more or less naked in Terra del Fuego, it is probable that from the Rissian Acheulean period onwards, man wore some sort of clothes. 'Scrapers' were no doubt used as knives to cut up animals or work wood, but they could also have served for rough work on skins and perhaps for making 'ponchos' for protection against wet and cold weather.

Were the Acheuleans nomadic, or partly settled? Certainly, like all the hunting peoples from a primitive level they must often have changed their encampments within a particular territory. But in certain caves it is possible to follow, sometimes over a depth of more than a metre, the evolution of the same Acheulean industry; and this shows that they had at any rate some permanent bases which they did not often leave, or to which they constantly returned.

From this period onwards there were no doubt cultural provinces. There is a striking difference between the classical Acheulean in the north of France (stretching down moreover as far as the Charente) and that of the open-air sites and caves in Périgord. Spanish Acheulean is more African than European. Even in Africa, though Acheulean with cleavers is dominant over a broad strip running from South Africa to Morocco, cleavers do not exist in Nubia and in Egypt. And eastern Europe would seem to have been in the hands of the Clactonians (in the broadest sense), who had outposts as far afield as France and England.

Parallel with the Acheulean, but certainly later than the Clactonian and perhaps derived from the latter or from certain Acheuleans, there was a development of non-handaxe industries which one can only call pre-Mousterian, for typologically they have Mousterian characters, and the word 'Tayacian' has never been clearly defined. In any case, this development included various industries, and it was these pre-Mousterian industries that were the origin of the various Mousterian assemblages.

AMB 39-41A-E
PHASE 1 SURF

At the beginning of the Würm period, whilst Acheulean still persisted in the form of Micoquian and allied industries, Mousterian was developing and spreading in an impressive manner from China to England and from Germany to the north of the Sahara. South of this desert, the Acheulean became transformed into forest Sangoan and steppe Fauresmith.

In Western Europe, the Mousterian complex in the strict sense developed along four main parallel lines which did not interfere with one another to any great extent. As we have seen, they no doubt had a variety of origins. The many interstratifications encountered in the deposits shows that we are dealing with different lines, and not as was formerly thought with an evolution (Acheulean-tradition Mousterian – typical Mousterian – upper Quina-type Mousterian). Nor does the idea that these differences represent seasonal activities any longer hold good. We now know

*Figure 49* (*Left, above*) Funeral pit of a very young child in the Lower Mousterian of Combe-Grenal (Dordogne). The stones which were placed over the small corpse are clearly visible. *Figure 50* (*Left, below*) General view of the funeral pit at Combe-Grenal. *Figure 51* (*Below*) Ground level plan of the Mousterian hut at Molodova I (western Russia), showing 1, hearths; 2, bones; 3, mammoth teeth.

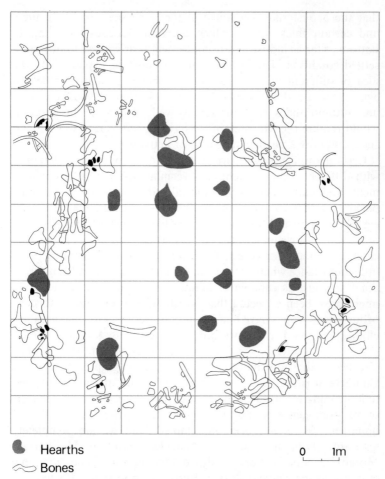

Hearths
Bones
Mammoth teeth

0     1m

that the Mousterians remained at the same site for a long time, and certain thick layers, which are homogeneous from top to bottom as far as industries are concerned, bear witness to this semi-settled condition. The notion that this could be explained by the idea of different winter and summer sheltering places comes up against the fact that there are four lines, so that we should have to add autumn and spring quarters as well. Moreover, this solution would require the Mousterians to have agreed to reserve such and such a site for a particular season or activity.

Certain anthropologists are reluctant to accept the idea that man with different industries could have inhabited the same environment, and that others with identical industries could have prospered in different environments. But this is nevertheless the case; e.g. North African Mousterian is very like French Mousterian. The influence of environment seems only to be paramount in extreme cases – in steppe or forest, for instance. But it appears to be of little importance whether the steppe is hot or cold, for a Mousterian point was just as capable of killing an antelope as a reindeer. It might have been expected that North African or Middle Eastern Mousterians would have had less need of scrapers for making their clothes; but that perhaps was only a subsidiary use for them.

An objection to the existence of these four Mousterian lines has also been raised on the score of a lack of geographical isolation. Contacts, it is said, must have been numerous, and must have led to a blending of cultures; the Mousterian physical type, moreover, seems homogeneous. But the Mousterian type is not really as homogeneous as has been maintained; and we are completely ignorant about man of the Acheulean-tradition Mousterian. Moreover, man is more ready to exchange his genes than his customs, as the whole history of Europe demonstrates. If a woman from the Quina-type Mousterian was carried off by an Acheulean-tradition Mousterian man, she may perhaps have continued to make her tribal type of thick scraper (scattered specimens of which are found in the Acheulean-tradition Mousterian), but after her death probably no one went on making them. And finally, it must always be remembered that the Palaeolithic world was an empty world. We must not unreservedly extend to the Mousterian period the observations recorded about primitive tribes in the world today. For one thing, the population was certainly very thin on the ground. Nor can we compare the Mousterians to the Australian aborigines or Bushmen, for the Mousterians no doubt wandered much less and so made even rarer contact with others. A man must often have lived and died without meeting anyone of another culture, although he knew 'that there are men living beyond the river who make handaxes'.

Passing beyond the boundaries of France, we find other types of Mousterian, e.g. Mousterian with foliated pieces in Germany, the Starocelie-Volgograd type in Russia, the Teshik Tash in Uzbekistan, etc., not to mention the industries in south-eastern Asia. Towards the south, in Spain, Mousterian with cleavers no doubt inherited this feature from the Acheulean, and extended a few tentative feelers into France as far as the Dordogne. In North Africa, it was typical Mousterian that seems to have prevailed, perhaps with a little of the Quina type. In the Middle East, the Mousterian sequence is complex. In Africa south of the Sahara, the Acheulean persisted in the form of derived industries.

It is in the Mousterian period that we come across the first traces of religious feeling in the form of intentional burials (figures 49 and 50), and perhaps in the 'cult of the bear'. This is an idea that has been strongly attacked, but which seems to be regaining favour since Bonifay's discovery of bear-burials in the Régourdou cave in the Dordogne. The presence of numerous fragments of red or black colouring matter in a good many sites shows that the Mousterians were already painting something – their own skin, leather or wood – since none of the parietal painting is certainly Mousterian. Sometimes, as at Pech de l'Azé, there have been discoveries of colour-grinding instruments. Finally, there is evidence of the first clear signs of arrangement in the habitat, such as paving at La Ferrassie, a post-hole at Combe-Grenal, and a hut-floor at Moldova, etc. (see figure 51).

Taken as a whole, the Mousterian stage is more diversified than the great Acheulean expansion which spread in uniform fashion over a large part of Africa, Europe and Asia. The Mousterian world with its increasing complexity was a prelude to the Upper Palaeolithic.

# 12 The Upper Palaeolithic in France

As far as the origins of modern man are concerned, the findings of anthropology and archaeology appear to contradict one another. The majority of Western anthropologists consider it unlikely that modern man is derived from the Neanderthal type. The anthropological differences are too great, and the time interval between them too short; moreover, the ancient Neanderthal men would seem to have been less specialised than the more recent ones. In fact these anthropologists take as the typical Neanderthal man the specimen found at La Chapelle aux Saints – the most specialised one known to us. We shall examine this problem more fully later on.

The first industries that could be called Upper Palaeolithic appear during the interstadial Würm II/III (I/II in the German chronology). This is the early Perigordian, sometimes called Châtelperronian or Castelperronian, from the cave at Châtelperron in the Allier district. It is difficult to give it an exact date, since the radiocarbon dating begins to become inaccurate at about this figure; but it would be at least 34 to 35,000 years before our era. Deposits of old Perigordian are relatively rare, perhaps because they belonged to an interstadial and were partly destroyed at the beginning of Würm III. Some good excavations have recently been carried out on these levels at Arcy-sur-Cure (Yonne) by Leroi-Gourhan; in the Trou de la Chèvre near Brantôme (Dordogne) by Jude and Arambourou; and at Les Cottés (Vienne) by Pradel, supplementing the older excavations at Châtelperron, Le Roc de Combe-Capelle, etc.

One of the characteristics of this old Perigordian is that its stone industry is still very strongly marked by Mousterian features. The finds include numerous and varied scrapers, Mousterian points, Levallois flakes, and Mousterian-style denticulates. And if one remembers that in the Acheulean-tradition Mousterian, backed knives tend in the final stages to be made of blades rather than flakes, and that end-scrapers and gravers are by no means rare, nor

*Figure 52 (Below)* Pierced teeth and bone pendants from the Lower Perigordian layer at Arcy-sur-Cure (Yonne, France). *Figure 53 (Right)* Bone awls from the same layer at Arcy-sur-Cure.

are borers and truncated blades, it becomes more and more difficult to avoid the conclusion that this lower Perigordian is derived from a local development of an Acheulean-tradition Mousterian in the Upper Palaeolithic. Moreover, the zones over which these industries are found coincide.

The tools which characterise the old Perigordian are essentially pointed blades with curved backs blunted by steep retouching, Châtelperron knives (figure 54, 1 to 5), often rather mediocre burins on a retouched truncation or dihedral butt, more often on a broken fragment, and end-scrapers often on flakes rather than on blades. Generally speaking, there is a paucity of bone implements except at Arcy, which seems to represent an already evolved level

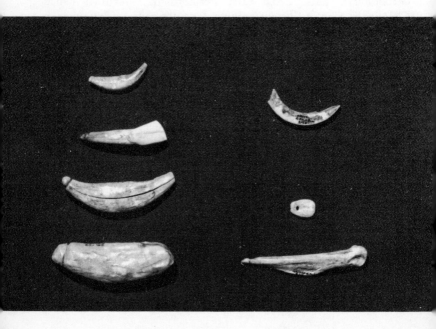

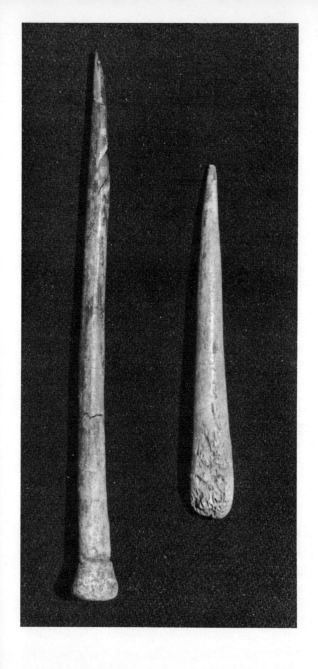

*Figure 54* Flint tools from the Perigordian. *Lower Perigordian.* 1, Chatelperron knife; 2, burin; 3, scraper on a flake; 4, Mousterian point; 5, denticulated and truncated blade (compare with figure 37). *Upper Perigordian.* 6, Gravette point; 7, multiple burin on truncation; 8, bitruncated blade; 9, Noailles burin; 10, backed bladelet; 11, truncated element; 12, flake scraper; 13, Font-Robert point; 14, dihedral burin. (1–5, Arcy-sur-Cure; 6, 7, 8, 10, 14, Corbiac, Dordogne; 9, Noailles; 11, Oreille d'Enfer, Les Eyzies; 12, La Gravette; 13, Laussel.)

since it belongs rather to the beginning of Würm III than to the interstadial. There are also bone awls, sometimes with heads, notched bones, teeth with grooves for suspension, and pendants of carved bone (see figures 52 and 53).

Up to about 1930, the idea of the evolution of Upper Palaeolithic in Western Europe followed Breuil's scheme: Early Aurignacian, with Châtelperron knives, Middle, with cleft-base bone points, and Upper, with La Gravette points. Peyrony divided this sequence into two different lines: Perigordian (Lower and Upper Aurignacian of Breuil), with five sub-divisions, and Aurignacian proper (Middle Aurignacian of Breuil), likewise divided into five. One of the principal objections advanced by Peyrony's opponents was that there was no continuity between the 'Castelperronian' and the 'Gravettian'. This argument seemed to gain in strength when it was observed that the Laugerie-Haute level, called by Peyrony 'Perigordian III' and thought by him to be intermediate, was in reality later than his Perigordian V. Moreover, his Perigordian II was really Aurignacian. But recent discoveries have supplied the continuity, for at Les Cottés (Vienne) Pradel discovered a Perigordian layer below some Aurignacian I (in the strict sense), which yielded more evolved implements than the traditional Early Perigordian and where it was possible to see the transition from the Châtelperron knife to the La Gravette point and in general the transition from the still primitive Early Perigordian implements to those of the Upper Perigordian. And this transition seems to have taken place early on, since this layer is earlier than Early Aurignacian.

We must in fact give up the 'instantaneous' conception of the Palaeolithic industries, a conception which still holds unconscious sway over the minds of many archaeologists. The old excavations, which hardly did any subdivision of levels, arrived at a 'global' representation of the industries. For example, all the levels with

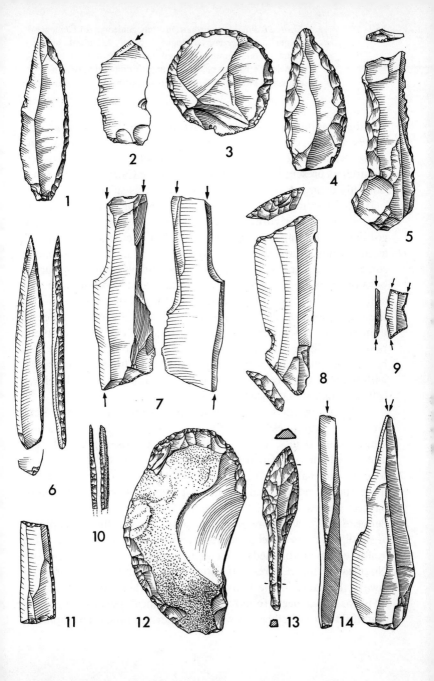

*Figure 55* Final Perigordian (Protomagdalenian) of Laugerie-Haute, at Les Eyzies, Dordogne. 1, borer; 2, multiple burin; 3 and 4, bone points; 5, pierced tooth; 6, denticulated backed bladelet; 7, backed bladelet; 8 and 10, dihedral burins on retouched blades; 9, double dihedral burin; 11, retouched blade.

split-base points were placed in Aurignacian 'ɪ', as though this represented a period of a few decades or centuries, when we are really dealing with a matter of thousands of years. The statistical research at present being carried out, and the Carbon[14] dating, will certainly change a good many opinions on this subject.

It would seem, then, that this Les Cottés level provides the link between Early Perigordian and what may be called Middle Perigordian or the La Gravette level. This last is characterised by the almost total disappearance of the Mousterian forms, although some side-scrapers persist and by the great development of burins, both on truncated blades – in which case they are often multiple – and 'bec de flûte' burins; by scrapers on the end of a blade although there is a special type of flake scraper; and by the existence of numerous flint points with abruptly retouched backs, La Gravette points of a large size, and smaller microgravettes. There are also backed bladelets, and sometimes small points, little foliated pieces with semi-abrupt retouch. In Peyrony's classification, this level was called Perigordian ɪv (see figure 54).

As for Perigordian v, it was subdivided into three levels. Perigordian va continues the Perigordian ɪv implements, but adds to it tanged flint points, called Font-Robert points (figure 54, 13), after a site in the Corrèze district. Their surface is sometimes covered with flat retouch. Perigordian vb saw the disappearance of those special points, and the development of truncated elements, backed blades truncated at one or both ends (figure 54, 11). Perigordian vc, while preserving the gravettes, saw the development of small burins as the characteristic tool. They were very flat, often multiple, on retouched truncated blades, and are known as Noailles burins (Corrèze) (figure 54, 9). Although the order is always the same in the two or three sites where these three subdivisions have been found in stratigraphical position, it seems doubtful today whether this was a single evolutionary development,

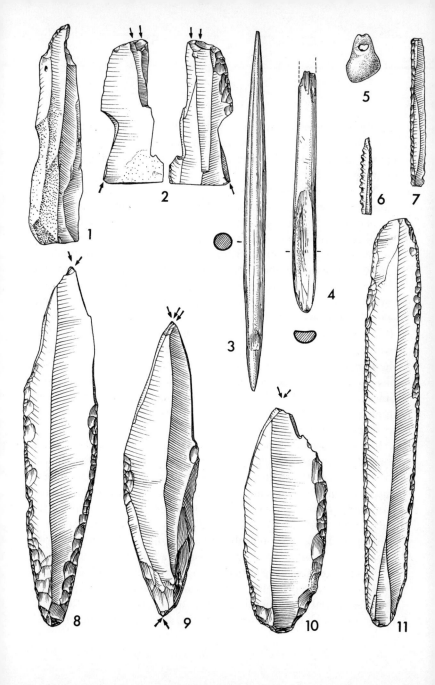

and the recent researches of Movius at the Abri Pataud appear to show that the level with Noailles gravers might represent a lateral branch of Perigordian, which is moreover represented in a number of other deposits.

Above the Noailles Perigordian, there has been found at the Abri Pataud at Les Eyzies a layer identical with the one which at Laugerie-Haute had been attributed to Middle Perigordian (III). It still contains Gravette points, though they are less numerous; the burins are of various kinds (from Middle Perigordian onwards they considerably outnumber the end-scrapers); and the principal characteristic is the development of blades (without chamfered backs), either truncated or bitruncated (see figure 54, 8). It would seem that the level which – at Laugerie-Haute too – had been called 'Protomagdalenian' by Peyrony because of engraving representing two mammoths face to face, should in fact be placed at the end of the Perigordian. Gravettes now become rare, but there are numerous backed bladelets (sometimes denticulate), fine burins, sometimes on retouched blades, borers, etc. End-scrapers are rare. Bone implements – which are rather few in the Perigordian – now begin to develop (see figure 55).

The Perigordian habitat is the same as for the Mousterian. It consists of caves, especially shelters, and extensive settlements in the open air. In the shelters at Arcy-sur-Cure, it has been possible to uncover the foundations of Early Perigordian huts (Leroi-Gourhan). In the Bergerac region, there are huge open-air settlements now being excavated by the Laboratoire de Préhistoire de Bordeaux. These will undoubtedly enable us to fill out our knowledge of the habitat with a good deal of additional detail.

The climate must have varied during the course of the Perigordian evolution. It was probably relatively mild at the beginning, during the interstadial II/III, then it became rapidly very cold, afterwards passing through more or less temperate fluctuations, one of which coincided with the Noailles level. In the final stage, conditions were again very cold.

According to our present information the Aurignacian – unlike the Perigordian – would not seem to have originated in western Europe, but to have arrived there ready-made, although there are likenesses between certain of its tools and others of the Quina-type Mousterian. It, too, may have been present in primitive form as early as the interstadial Würm II/III, but the Aurignacian developed mainly in the glacial climate of the early Würm III. Its implements are very different from those of the Perigordian, consisting of fine blade types, often with bold scalar retouch; scrapers on the end of this type of blade; burins – rare at first, but then developing, though never reaching the same proportions as in the Perigordian; special end-scrapers on thick flakes or small blocks, achieved by means of delicate thin-flake (lamelliform) retouching, either carinated or nose-shaped (figure 56, 1,3). It is this kind of thick end-scraper that is reminiscent of the Quina-type Mousterian (they are in fact met with sporadically from the Riss period onwards, at La Micoque for instance). Certain retouched blades – the so-called strangled blades – are characteristic of the Early Aurignacian, although they are always relatively rare. The bone implements (awls, *bâtons de commandements* or pierced antler bars, smoothing-tools etc.), are in particular characterised by flat elongated spearheads, more or less triangular and with a cleft base, representing a first attempt at fitting over a handle but subsequently given up probably on account of its fragility. These split-base points constitute the type-fossil for Aurignacian I. The Aurignacian evolution consists of the progressive abandonment of the fine retouched blades, a development of burins, the respective variation of the proportion of carinated and nose-scrapers, as well as their general percentage. Aurignacian II, enjoying a definitely less cold climate, developed new bone points, lozenge-shaped and flattened,

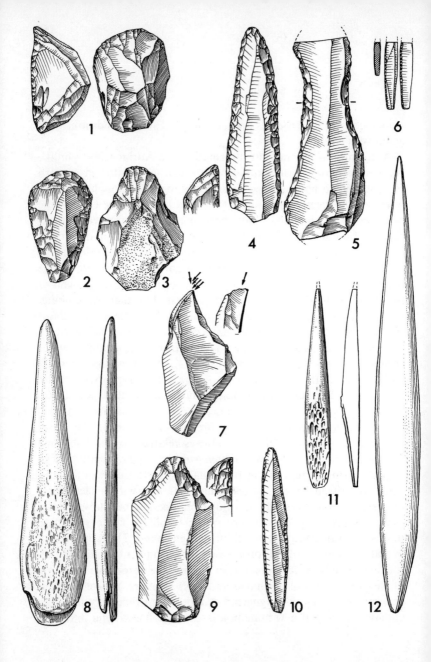

without a split-base, which had already made their appearance in certain Aurignacian I deposits. Among the burins there is now a special type, the busked burin, in which several narrow bladelets, stopped by a notch, are removed to form a convex chisel edge. This is the type-fossil for this phase of the Aurignacian. Aurignacian III has stone implements without very much change (though with a smaller percentage of busked burins), and lozenge-shaped oval-section points instead of flat ones. Aurignacian IV has bone points that are round in section and biconical; and Aurignacian V – coming in at the end and rather late, since it is later than the final Perigordian (Protomagdalenian) at Laugerie-Haute – has simple bevel-base bone points and is fairly rich in burins. This last stage is seen to be related to the Aurignacian by the great development of carinated end-scrapers, sometimes denticulate, and nose-scrapers.

At various levels and in varying proportions we meet with small bladelet tools, with small, semi-abrupt and alternate retouch, called Dufour bladelets (figure 56, 6), from the Corrèze site where they were defined. They have been formerly and wrongly considered characteristic of certain Perigordian stages. In the whole of the Aurignacian development there are (with very rare exceptions) no implements with chamfered backs, although there are some Châtelperron knives in the lower levels (were these simply picked up, or do they represent convergences or influences?).

In a fairly Early Aurignacian level at Font-Yves (Corrèze) there are small elongated points, more or less leaf-shaped, and likewise semi-abruptly retouched artifacts known as the Font-Yves points (see figure 56, 10).

The Aurignacian and Perigordian people seem to have lived 'side by side' during the Würm III period, without influencing each other to any greater extent than the various Mousterians did during Würm I and II. It is interesting to note that the deposits of the Lower Perigordian are relatively rare and those of the Early

Aurignacian relatively abundant. The opposite is true for the upper stages of these two industries. There is every indication that the environment in which the Early Perigordian was in course of developing was then invaded by a wave of Aurignacian, which was later to ebb.

Towards the end of Würm III, after the final Perigordian and Aurignacian, the sequence seems to have been interrupted by the Solutrean intrusion. It would appear that this new culture could not take root – at least not directly – either in the Aurignacian or in the Perigordian. And a young Canadian archaeologist, Philip Smith, has recently published a masterly book (*Le Solutréen en France*) in which he effectively disposes of the theories that saw the origin of this Solutrean in North Africa or central Europe. Its origin is in fact still a mystery. Perhaps the solution is to be found in a prolonged Mousterian, such as seems to exist in Provence.

Solutrean (see figure 57) begins with a primitive stage, called Protosolutrean, of which there are a few known deposits, the principal one being at Laugerie-Haute (Dordogne). The implements comprise many more end-scrapers than gravers, and the characteristic type is a leaf-shaped flint point with one plane face and the other retouched. It is often delicately retouched only on the dorsal face, except for a few retouches removing part of the bulb. In addition, there are Mousterian-style implements, such as side-scrapers, discs, etc. This Protosolutrean passes over into a more evolved Solutrean, in which the uni-facial point remains, however, the characteristic implement. Towards the end, the retouching of the points tends to become bifacial and we find ourselves fairly suddenly in Middle Solutrean, which is characterised by a large number of leaf-shaped pieces, often very fine, with complete bifacial retouching: the so-called laurel-leaves. They are very variable in dimensions, and must have served for a number of uses as implements, the smaller ones as missiles, the medium as knives, the large ones as ritual objects or 'works of art', often reaching extreme proportions and great delicacy, for instance at Le Volgu (Saône-et-Loire), (35 cm by 8·8 cm by 0·9 cm). The majority of these specimens were chipped by direct percussion; but for the finer ones, indirect percussion or pressure has been used. There are some indications that the Solutreans sometimes used to treat flint by means of heat, which makes pressure-flaking easier.

During the Würm III/IV interstadial, the Upper Solutrean developed. It is marked by the appearance of two new types: shouldered points and willow-leaves, usually worked by means of pressure. But laurel-leaves and unifacial points still continue to be produced. In France there are also some stemmed and barbed points. Taken as a whole, the Solutrean flint implements, with their relatively rare burins, plentiful end-scrapers, a fairly high percentage of borers, and the presence – especially at the beginning – of Mousterian forms, presents a rather static picture, apart from its characteristic stone points. In the Upper Solutrean, however, there is a tendency to extend Solutrean retouching to other types of tool, especially to the end-scrapers. Up to this point, bone implements have been poorly represented; but in the Upper Solutrean they too undergo development. The first eyed needles also make their appearance. The radiocarbon method has furnished three datings for the Lower Solutrean at Laugerie-Haute, ranging from 18 to 19,000 years before our era.

This brilliant Solutrean culture, which carried flint-working to one of its highest levels, suddenly disappeared in somewhat mysterious circumstances. The oldest Magdalenian levels often overlie the Solutrean without a break, so much so that it is difficult to trace the dividing-line between these two levels except by the typology. But within the limits of what we know about the Palaeolithic culture, it is impossible to think that the one culture might have evolved into the other. The implements are completely

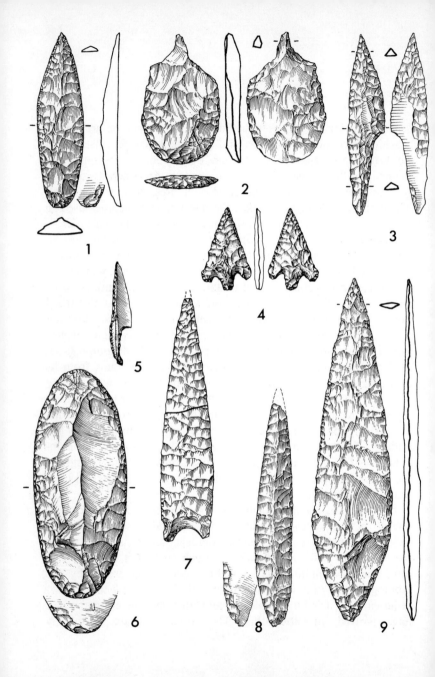

*Figure 57 Lower Solutrean.* 1, leaf-shaped point with one flat face;
6, finely retouched end-scraper. *Middle Solutrean.* 2, borer end-scraper on a
broken laurel leaf. *Upper Solutrean.* 3, shouldered point; 9, laurel leaf;
8, willow leaf; 7, point with a concave base. *Spanish Solutrean.* 4, tanged
and barbed point; 5, shouldered point. (1,6,8, Laugerie-Haute; 3,9, Fourneau
du Diable, Dordogne; 7, Lespugue, Haute Garonne; 4,5, Parpallo, Spain.)

different; and if the Solutrean represents one of the zeniths of stone-chipping, the lowest Magdalenian is certainly one of its nadirs.

We do not know the cause of this abrupt disappearance: it may have been due to invasions, wars, or epidemics. Future research may perhaps provide the basis for a plausible hypothesis.

The evolution of the Solutrean as outlined above applies to the classical zone of Périgord – Charente. Outside this zone, the development was rather different. At the eponymous site of Solutré near Macon (Saône-et-Loire), the Upper Solutrean is characterised by fine unifacial points, with the same kind of retouch as the meridional shouldered points, which caused the Abbé Breuil to call them the '*pointes à cran sans cran*'. In the Rhône valley the Lower Solutrean is well represented, whilst the Middle Solutrean is rare and the Upper Solutrean is replaced by an industry with small shouldered points clearly differing from the classic type, and by microliths. There is at present some doubt whether this industry represents a special evolution of Solutrean or the advent of another culture. In the Landes there is a Solutrean industry at Montaut with a special kind of laurel-leaves, having a more or less pronounced shoulder; and at Brassempouy – as in the Pyrenees – the Upper Solutrean carries some Spanish forms, as well as the classic shouldered points, particularly points with a concave base (see figure 57, 7).

Except perhaps for some faint and dubious traces, Solutrean does not exist in France east of the Rhône, and does not in any case spread over into central Europe. It is essentially a western culture.

The oldest Magdalenian, as met with for instance at Laugerie-Haute below Magdalenian I, is obscure in its origins. The almost complete absence of back-blunted specimens, blades or bladelets prevents us from seeking its source in the Perigordian, in spite of the presence of numerous transverse burins which exist in the Upper Perigordian and also in Aurignacian V. The technique is crude and

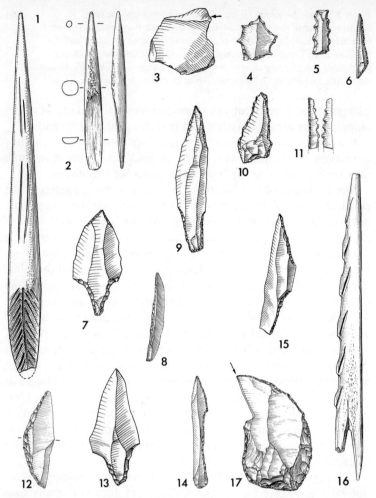

the implements are often shaped from flakes rather than made on blades. There are prototypes of little side-scrapers with very abrupt retouch often all round the edge (*raclettes*) and star-shaped borers. The almost complete absence of carinated end-scrapers makes it difficult to derive it directly from Aurignacian v, in spite of some 'echoes' of Aurignacian such as retouched or even strangled blades, which are unfortunately very rare in the final Aurignacian. There

is an appreciable percentage of splintered pieces and the bone
implements include some large reindeer-antler spears.

Although little is known about the origins of this Magdalenian
'O', its line of descent can be seen in the Magdalenian I that follows
it (see figure 58). Burins are developing, but the percentage of
transverse burins diminishes. As in the preceding level, there are
some carinated end-scrapers or nose-scrapers. The characteristic
tools are the little *raclettes*, star-shaped borers – or anyway multiple
ones – and splintered pieces. The bone implements are well
developed with several types of javelin bone-points, the most
characteristic of which has a simple slightly convex bevel decorated
with a chevron motif. Needles, pierced *bâtons* and smoothing-tools
complete the series of bone implements. Note the extreme rarity
of chamfered-back specimens among the implements of stone.

There then comes in a second discontinuity, for Magdalenian II
does not appear to follow on logically. Thick end-scrapers are few
in number, and the *raclettes* almost disappear. On the other hand
the bladelet implements develop considerably, and there are backed
and sometimes denticulate bladelets, as well as scalene triangles
(figure 58, 6). There is a bone industry, often made of red deer
antler (for we are now in the middle of the Würm III/IV interstadial);
and it produces quite clearly different bone-points, either biconical
or roughly bevelled.

Magdalenian III, which follows on, is equally rich in backed
bladelets, and still includes some triangles. Raclettes are also
present in by no means negligible percentage. Bone implements
are well developed, the typical pieces being a javelin bone-point,
often short and with a long simple bevelled base, or elongated and
grooved points. There are wands with semi-circular cross-section,
sometimes with decorations. Taken as a whole, Magdelanian III
seems to follow on naturally from Magdalenian II but shows some
influence of Magdalenian I.

164

*Figure 59* From left to right,
two Magdalenian V harpoons with a single row
of barbs, two Magdalenian VI harpoons
with a double row of barbs,
an Azilian harpoon with perforated base.

From Magdalenian III onwards – that is, from the end of the interstadial – the flint instruments, including many and various burins, do not undergo any further important modifications except for the appearance of some special types at the end of Magdalenian v and in Magdalenian vi (figure 58, 7, 14, 17). As far as bone implements are concerned, Magdalenian iv sees the appearance of the first prototype harpoons, in the shape of points with tentative and sketchy barbs (figure 58, 18); with them are found awls, smoothing tools, semi-circular wands often with a geometric decoration. The javelin bone-points have simple bevelled bases, or sometimes in the form of a quadrangular pyramid. There are some spear-throwers, and numerous works of art.

Magdalenian v has harpoons with a single row of barbs sticking well out from the shaft (figure 59), tridents, bone-points with a simple bevelled or quadrangular base, more often with a double and sometimes striated bevel. Among the stone implements there are some very long shouldered points, with short heads, and gravette points crop up again.

Magdalenian vi is sometimes divided into via, with harpoons armed with a double row of rounded barbs, and vib, in which they are angular (figure 59). There is a continuance of harpoons with a single row of barbs. In the stone implements a special type of burin makes its appearance called the 'parrot-beak' burin; but it hardly exists outside the south-west of France. There are also other special types (figure 58, 7): tanged points, differing from the Font-Robert Perigordian and known as Teyjat or Font-Brunel points; leaf-shaped points with delicate marginal and sometimes alternate retouch, called Laugerie-Basse points. There are curved-back knives rather reminiscent of the Châtelperrons (azilian points), and the little short end-scrapers often shaped like a thumb-nail which are a prelude to the Azilian. In certain sites geometric microliths appear and develop, such as triangles, trapezes and semi-lunates.

As well as harpoons, the bone implements comprise needles, smoothing-tools etc., and javelin bone-points, exceptionally with a simple bevel base. Usually there is a double bevel, and the section of the shaft is sometimes quadrangular. The spear-throwers seem to have disappeared: could this possibly be because the bow had been invented?

The Upper Magdalenian brings the Ice Age to an end. The Azilian, which then follows, belongs to the post-glacial period, but still belongs in reality to the Upper Palaeolithic, a Palaeolithic that adapted itself to very changed conditions. Forest development was not favourable to man, and the powerful Magdalenian tribes split up into little groups. The implements fall off considerably in quality and become reduced to a few types: flake end-scrapers, thumb-nail scrapers and azilian points. Burins become rare. Bone implements consist mainly of flat red deer-antler harpoons, the base being pierced with a hole (figure 59), and of awls. Art, which had developed so splendidly in the Magdalenian, is now limited to pebbles engraved or painted with geometrical designs.

# 13 The Upper Palaeolithic in western and central Europe

The series is for most of the time far from being as complete as in south-western France; truth to tell, there are already some gaps even in France, apart from certain favoured regions.

In Belgium there is an Early Aurignacian industry with split-base points in various places (Montaigle, Trou Magrite, Spy, etc.). There may also be some Aurignacian II. The Early Perigordian is unknown, and the Upper Perigordian is of Perigordian V type. At Trou Magrite there was a level of Font-Robert points, and likewise at Spy. At Goyet there were some large truncated elements and at least one typical Noaille burin. At Engis there are some truncated elements. No Solutrean exists in Belgium, although it has sometimes been erroneously identified. Magdalenian is solely represented by the Upper Magdalenian at Goyet, at Font-de-Forêt, and especially at Trou de Chaleux. This presents an oriental facies, nearer to the west German or Swiss than to the south-western French type, especially in the abundance of its borers. This northeastern influence makes itself even more strongly felt in the final Palaeolithic or in the Epipalaeolithic. The deposit at Lommel, wrongly attributed to a late survival of the Perigordian, is in fact an Epimagdalenian belonging to the northern plains. The important gaps in the series do not seem to be due to the climate, for as far as the Lower Perigordian and Solutrean – Early Magdalenian periods are concerned, they correspond to a period of milder conditions.

In Switzerland only Magdalenian is represented. Man would seem to have followed the retreating glaciers. The sites are to be found either in the Geneva region or round about Basle or Schaffhausen, where the Kesslerloch cave has yielded a justly famous reindeer drawing and implements which probably stretch from Magdalenian IV to VI. This Swiss Magdalenian, like the Belgian, contains many borers, and among the smaller objects some flint rectangles.

In Germany, Châtelperron knives have been reported at Ofnet (Bavaria), and at Ranis (Thuringia). The Upper Perigordian probably exists at various places. There is magnificent testimony to the Aurignacian at the Vogelherd site in Würtemberg (excavations by Professor Riek). On top of some older levels is a layer attributed to Aurignacian I, for there are numerous split-base bone-points and some fine delicately retouched blades. But it differs from the French Aurignacian by its richness in burins and its poverty in carinated end-scrapers. This layer has also produced a fine series of animal statuettes, which are among the oldest known to us. Above this there is a second Aurignacian layer, with no split-base points and rather more carinated end-scrapers and nose-scrapers; but it is difficult to see its kinship with Aurignacian II, for there is a notable complete absence of busked burins. This German Aurignacian is met with in other deposits, and in north-west Germany near the Rhine the Wildhaus cave has produced a fine lozenge-shaped bone-point reminiscent of those belonging to Aurignacian II in France.

We should remind ourselves that a part of the industry containing *Blattspitzen* seems to belong to the Upper Palaeolithic age, and might be connected with the Hungarian Szeletian.

Solutrean is completely lacking. Lower Magdalenian has not been identified with any certainty. Upper Magdalenian is present at a good number of sites. The Petersfels cave north-west of Lake Constance is connected with the neighbouring Swiss sites. In the loess near Andernach on the Rhine there is Magdalenian VI with harpoons having one or two rows of barbs.

In northern Germany, there is the Hamburgian industry, contemporary with Magdalenian but rather different from it. It is characterised by end-scrapers on blades with small side retouch, numerous borers, some of them with large lop-sided points (*Zinken*), very few burins, and especially by the Hamburgian points, which are shouldered points obliquely truncated (figure 58, 15). There are some fairly big geometrical flints, but few or no backed blade-lets. Alongside this evolving Hamburgian there are industries with more or less Magdalenian affinities, generally rather late in developing. This Epimagdalenian is divided into several groups (H. Schwabedissen). In the final Palaeolithic may also be placed Ahrensburgian, which is no doubt descended from the Hambur-gian. It is characterised by tanged points (figure 58, 9) probably derived from the Hamburgian point. It is difficult to trace a dividing line between final Palaeolithic and Mesolithic, for man continued the Palaeolithic way of life well on into the postglacial period.

In Denmark the final Palaeolithic is represented by the Bromme industry in the island of Seeland. It probably dates from the Alleröd oscillation towards the end of the ice age, and would appear to be related to the Ahrensburgian by reason of its tanged points (figure 58, 13).

In Holland, the Upper Palaeolithic is represented by the Tjonger group, belonging to the northern Epimagdalenian studied by Schwabedissen and characterised by points that are often broken-backed and by short end-scrapers which are thumb-nail-shaped or circular in the final stages.

In England, Upper Palaeolithic industries are rare and usually poor in implements. There have been discoveries of Aurignacian (?), particularly at Paviland (Wales). Lower Solutrean has also been mentioned; but as in Belgium, it is really a question of implements with flat retouching on the lower face, akin rather to certain Polish industries. At Kent's Cavern in Devonshire and at Aveline Hole in the south-west of England there were industries producing har-poons with one or two rows of barbs, together with backed blades of a more or less Azilian type, eyed needles, etc. According to Schwabedissen, this 'Cresswellian' is related to the Tjonger group in Holland and might even be its ancestor.

In Spain, Upper Palaeolithic is both varied and abundant. The

Reclau-Viver cave in Catalonia has yielded traces of Early Perigordian, and this is the only certain remains of it in the Iberian Peninsula; then there is a level of scanty but typical Aurignacian, with split-base bone-points. Above this comes an Upper Perigordian, poor in burins (which is exceptional) but rich in gravettes. The Solutrean above it is unusual, for it has lopsided tanged laurelleaves and peculiar shouldered points. At La Bora Gran, there is Magdalenian with harpoons having two rows of barbs, identical with the French Magdalenian.

The Cantabrian region and the Basque country have produced a series of important sites. At Castillo the Mousterian was covered by typical Aurignacian with split-base points, carinated scrapers, etc., several levels of Perigordian with gravettes, Solutrean with laurelleaves, then Magdalenian which has been taken to be Old but which is certainly Middle, and finally Upper Magdalenian with only one row of barbs on the perforated based harpoons, and some Azilian. In other places, the Magdalenian has been labelled 'III', for it has no harpoons but does contain Azilian points. Upper Magdalenian with harpoons having a double row of barbs is known at a variety of sites.

The Solutrean in Cantabria seems to correspond only to Middle and especially Upper Solutrean. Alongside the French types found in the Dordogne, it comprises of leaf-shaped points, with convex or concave or sometimes asymmetrical bases (figure 57, 7). Azilian is well represented, particularly at Valle.

In the Spanish Levant south of Valencia, the Parpalló cave has yielded an interesting sequence. At the bottom there was a level with gravette points, then Solutrean levels with laurel-leaves. Above this tanged and barbed points began to appear – not unknown in the French Solutrean, but extremely rare. Here there is an abundance of them. They would appear to be accompanied by a special kind of shouldered point, in which the rim is defined by little steep retouches which do not cover the upper part of the point (figure 57, 4, 5). This was followed by Magdalenian I, with bone-points similar to those in French Magdalenian I; by Magdalenian II, unlike the French Magdalenian II; then by Magdalenian III, with numerous long-bevelled bone-points often geometrically decorated; and finally by Magdalenian IV, with prototype harpoons, in which there is said to be a development of geometric microliths. In various layers there were numerous engravings on small slabs (excavations by Professor Pericot).

Further south still, near Velez Blanco, the Cueva de Ambrosio (excavated by Ripoll Perelló) has yielded Solutrean levels with laurel-leaves, above which come levels with tanged and barbed points, and above these again are levels containing Parpalló-type tanged points. As in the case of the Rhône valley, there is the problem of deciding whether these tanged points belong to a special Upper Solutrean or to another industry.

Little is known of the Upper Palaeolithic in Portugal. There is some rather special Aurignacian, some Solutrean with classic shouldered points, Solutrean with tanged and barbed points, and perhaps some Upper Magdalenian.

In Italy there are the Grimaldi caves near the French frontier, where there was some Aurignacian material overlaid by various levels containing backed blades; but they were unfortunately explored at too early a date. Quite close to this is the Mochi shelter, recently excavated by A. C. Blanc and Cardini. At the bottom it yielded a layer of the general Aurignacian type and an important series of Dufour bladelets. It is followed by a distinctively Aurignacian level and a level that appears to be Upper Perigordian with gravettes and especially microgravettes, with burins tending to the Noailles type plus some other peculiar tools. This is probably a Mediterranean facies of the Perigordian. The same is true of the succeeding levels, which are rich in geometric microliths.

In northern Italy there appear to be some more or less Perigordian-like industries. There are industries with typical Noailles burins, microgravettes and unifacial leaf-shaped points in the Arno valley. In Latium, the Fossellone cave has yielded a typical Aurignacian industry, although it is chipped from pebbles. It contains split-base points, carinated scrapers and nose-scrapers, retouched blade scrapers, burins, etc., and has sometimes been called Circean (from Mount Circeo, where the cave lies). In the Otranto district the Romanelli cave has produced over a Quina-type Mousterian an industry with small backed points, pointed and sometimes leaf-shaped blades, small and not very distinct shouldered points, microliths, and in particular numerous small thumb-nail or short end-scrapers. An old interpretation of the stratigraphy had led to the ascription of this industry to the Early Upper Palaeolithic, whereas it is probably contemporary with the Magdalenian. It also contains some fine bone-points.

In Sicily – especially on the north coast – there are a fair number of Upper Palaeolithic deposits with backed implements that seem to be rather late (R. Vaufrey).

There are some celebrated deposits in Austria, especially in the loess, for example at Willendorf, where the famous female statuette was found.

There is an Early Aurignacian industry, with bone-points known as 'Mladec' or 'Lautsch' points, reminiscent of those in the French Aurignacian II, which are of large size, almost lozenge-shaped, and not split in the base. It is found in a number of caves, particularly at Repolust. A so-called 'recent' Aurignacian is to be found, particularly in the loess sites. At Krems it contains finely retouched Aurignacian blades, end-scrapers on Aurignacian blades, strangled blades, carinated scrapers, burins, and an important group of retouched bladelets, some of which are Dufour bladelets whilst others are retouched on the backs, and the retouching, which is sometimes very delicate, becomes steeper and more incisive. This last type passes over into the true backed blade, which would thus seem to have been re-invented independently of the Perigordians. There are also some Krems points, sometimes resembling the true Font-Yves and sometimes the 'oriental' Font-Yves from the Palestine sites.

At Willendorf II the lower layers (2 and 4) seem to be Aurignacian; layers 5 to 8 have been called 'Gravettian', but the Gravettian elements would appear to be doubtful. Layer 9 would seem to belong to the oriental Gravettian (Middle and Upper Perigordian), for it contains a special kind of shouldered point with a broad blade, of the same type as that of the upper layer of Kostienki I in Russia. By reason of its gravettes and truncated pieces, this layer certainly seems to belong to the Perigordian cycle in the broad sense of the term.

There is no Solutrean in Austria, but there is some Magdalenian material.

Czechoslovakia possesses a more varied Upper Palaeolithic. The oldest industry is probably the Szeletian, which seems to take the place of the Lower Perigordian and to extend into Aurignacian times. It is probably derived from a *Blattspitzen* Mousterian, but its evolution is still imperfectly understood. It is characterised by leaf-shaped points that are totally or partly bifacial, associated in varying proportions with Levallois flakes, numerous side-scrapers, end-scrapers, smaller quantities of burins, borers, some objects in the Aurignacian style, and some atypical backed pieces. Formerly – basing the evidence on the leaf-shaped pieces – it was thought that the Solutrean came from central Europe. There are about thirty Szeletian deposits in Czechoslovakia.

Very little is known of the Old Aurignacian: the best deposit would seem to be at Barca in Slovakia. The recent Aurignacian is better represented (at Nova Dedina for instance) and sometimes includes some Szeletian elements, which had been probably picked

*Figure 60* (*Left*) Sculpture representing a woman, from Dolni Vestonice.
*Figure 61* (*Below*) Sculpture representing a human head, also from Dolni Vestonice.

176    *Figure 62 Upper Perigordian* from Dolni Vestonice.
1, burin; 2, burin-scraper 3, multiple burin; 4, end-scraper
on retouched blade; 5,6, denticulated backed bladelets; 8, pointed
retouched blade; 9, 10, gravette points. *Szeletian* from Hungary.
7,11, bifacial foliate points. (7, from Miskolc; 11, from Szeleta cave.)

up. The Mladec (or Lautsch) cave has yielded some big lozenge-shaped bone-points.

The Perigordian seems only to be represented by already evolved, although sometimes relatively old, forms. In the loess, the site of Dolni Vestonice in Southern Moravia is one of the most important in central Europe. It has been known a long while, but the recent excavations have been very ably published by B.Klima. The most striking feature about this industry is the extent to which, in spite of the distance, it resembles the Upper Perigordian of western Europe; it may even perhaps be an easterly outpost of it (figures 60, 61, 62). This industry has been dated by Carbon[14] to 23,650 ± 170 years before our era. There are fairly plentiful bone implements, some ornamental pieces and clay figurines. The nearby site at Pavlov is dated 2 8 0 ± 150 years before our era, and has produced a slightly different industry, closer to those of Russia, which it has been proposed to call Pavlovian. In Slovakia, the deposit at Moravany bad Váhom–Podkovica has yielded gravettes and points of the Kostienki I–Willendorf type.

There is no Solutrean. The Magdalenian deposits are confined to the caves in the Moravian karst country. There have been perhaps three stages in what appears to be Upper Magdalenian. Taken as a whole, it is rich in borers, like the German. Swiss and Belgian. It includes many backed bladelets, sometimes bitruncated (rectangles) and various bone-points. The deposit at Pekarna has produced a fine harpoon with a double row of barbs, and some works of art.

The great site at Predmost in Moravia, which was excavated too early, did undoubtedly contain Aurignacian, Szeletian and 'Gravettian' with Kostienki I – Willendorf points.

In Hungary the Herman-Otta cave in the Bükk Mountains is said to have yielded some backed points 'of the Audi or Châtelperron type'. The Szeletian (figure 62, 7,11) derives its name from

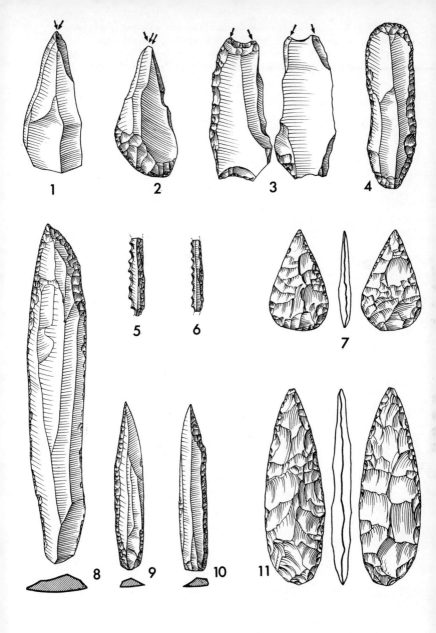

*Figure 63* Geographical position of Palaeolithic sites in Central and Eastern Europe. 1, Ahrensburg; 2, Petersfels; 3, Vogelherd; 4, Kesslerloch; 5, Schweizerbild; 6, Willendorf; 7,8, Dolni-Vistonice and Pavlov; 9, Predmost; 10, Wylotne; 11, Vertesszollös; 12, Tata; 13, Subalyuk; 14, Szeleta;

15, Istállóskö; 16, Voronovitsa; 17, Babin;
18, Moldova I and V; 19, Mezin; 20, Avdeyevo; 21, Sunghir;
22, Gagarino; 23, Kostienki group; 24, Volgograd;
25, Kammenaya Balka; 26, Starocelie; 27, Kiik-Koba; 28, Siuren.

the Szeleta cave, in the Bükk Mountains. The lower layer contains some blades, some burins and poor leaf-shaped bifacial specimens which have been crushed on their edges by natural action. The upper level, which is undisturbed, includes blades, end-scrapers, Mousterian-looking side-scrapers, backed blades and bladelets, and backed blades tending towards the gravette type. The leaf-shaped artifacts are well made and finer, in the form of a more or less elongated laurel-leaf; but the retouching is more reminiscent of the Mousterian than of the Solutrean.

In various deposits Szeletian material is accompanied by rare split-base bone points, which may simply testify to its being contemporary with Early Aurignacian. Vértes is of the opinion that the Szeletians used special bone tools to mine the deposits of ochre in the Lovas caves near Lake Balaton.

Aurignacian is met with in a variety of sites, the most important being at Istállóskö, also in the Bükk Mountains. The lower layer contained some fifty not very typical flints, including some thick end-scrapers and a fragment of a retouched blade; but there were no burins. Yet the bone implements are typically Aurignacian I, with numerous points – about twenty with split bases – varying from two to twenty centimetres in length, and several perforated pendants. The richer upper layer contains numerous Aurignacian blades, sometimes pointed, and reminiscent of those at Vogelherd. There are no carinated or nose-scrapers; the end-scrapers are short, and on retouched blades; there are hardly any burins, and those found are of poor quality. Side-scrapers are fairly plentiful, and there is a fragment of a fine Szeletian point. The bone industry is characterised by more or less lozenge-shaped points of large dimensions (Mladec or Olchewa points). Carbon[14] dating gives a figure of $28,760 \pm 600$ BC. The lower layer is certainly older, but Vértes's estimate of about 36,000 years seems too high. The fauna comprises more particularly remains of the cave bear, suggesting

*Figure 64* Bone points from the Aurignacian of Istállóskö (Hungary).

that this may have been a hunting site. The Pesko cave a few kilometres away seems to have yielded a similar stratigraphy.

It appears that 'oriental Gravettian' occurs on the plains (in connection with mammoth and reindeer-hunting). Gabori distinguished between two groups, one in southern Hungary connected with the oriental Gravettian, the other – in the Danube loess – more akin to the product of the Czechoslovakian or Austrian sites. To judge what has been published, it seems doubtful whether the majority of these industries can be 'Gravettian', unless the term be taken in such a wide sense that it loses all meaning. One is tempted to come back to the old classification and to see these industries as akin to the Magdalenian in the broad sense. If the early date proposed for them is accurate, it must be an industry all on its own which should be given a special name.

The very poor finds in the Pilisszanto shelter ii are attributed by Vértes to the Magdalenian.

In Yugoslavia there appears to be Aurignacian at the Mokriska jama site, for it has produced a split-base point and another triangular one. There are also some ill-defined industries in the Red Cave.

# 14 The Upper Palaeolithic in eastern Europe

In Poland the Upper Palaeolithic seems to make an early start with a strange industry, probably transitional, found in the Nietoperzowa cave at Jermanovice. The lower layer (layer 6) has been dated by Carbon[14] to about 36,000 years before our era. It has more particularly yielded a variety of leaf-shaped points, some being bifacial, reminiscent of laurel-leaves, and other more characteristic ones which are only bifacially retouched on the base and the point, or only on the base (figure 65, 1,6,7). In addition there were some flakes, cores, and used blades. Layer 5 is poorer still; layer 4 has produced a backed specimen like a short stout gravette, with flakes and points of the preceding type and a tendency for the point to be tanged. This layer 4 would appear to be definitely late, according to Chmielewski, and would belong about to the beginning of Würm IV (by French chronology), whilst the others date from the extreme beginning of Würm III or even the preceding interstadial.

At Piekary II, near the Vistula, there is an industry with Aurignacian characteristics (carinated end-scrapers, blades, etc.). The industry at Gora Pulawska, which is a little later, has some fine carinated scrapers, retouched blades, and bladelets recalling the Dufour or Krems type. There has sometimes been talk of the Aurignacian in the Mammoutova cave, and mention has been made of a non-existent split-base point. There were six hearths one above the other, but their industries became mixed after the excavator's death. The general impression is rather of the Perigordian, judging by the style of the burins (which are often multiple), the backed pieces, and the microgravettes. There were a series of ivory points, one of which was biconical.

It looks as though a Magdalenian 'III' or later industry existed in the Maszycka cave. Then after a gap there is a very marked development of an advanced or final Upper Palaeolithic industry, belonging to the Masovian or Tarnovian cycle. The Masovian which is contemporary with advanced Magdalenian in the west, is characterised by 'willow-leaf' points, often with flat retouching on the basal end and very little or no retouch on the other (figure 74, 7). There are burins, and end-scrapers, and the points are inclined to be tanged (Swiderian). Then comes the Pludian, or Middle Masovian, dating from the Alleröd oscillation and the beginning of the Upper Dryas. It has very short end-scrapers, fewer burins, and clearly tanged points. The Upper Masovian, contemporary with the end of the Upper Dryas, has very short end-scrapers, very rare burins, and points with more elongated tangs, some of which are reminiscent of the Ahrensburgian points.

Contemporary with the Middle Masovian is the Tarnovian. It has very short end-scrapers, some circular scrapers, some burins, and a very few backed pieces recalling the Azilian points. The Witovian – which is known from one single site – dates from the end of the Alleröd. It contains scrapers reminding one of the Tarnovian, points shaped like the segment of a circle and some very rare tanged points, reminiscent of those in Denmark but different from the Masovian points. In addition to these different industries there are some sites belonging to the group of Epimagdalenian industries from the northern plains.

From Rumania there have been reports of Szeletian assemblages, but the leaf-shaped specimens are more reminiscent of Russian types than of those found in Hungary or Czechoslovakia. The same is true of Bulgaria. The Aurignacian is said to exist in Rumania, with at least one bone-point of the Mladec-Olchewa type in the Baïa de Fier cave. In Bulgaria in 1912, a split-base bone-point was found in the Morowitza cave. Džambazow has found others in the Pest cave. Before the last war, Garrod found in the Bacho-Kiro cave some retouched blades, two burins, a bone-point (or awl); and lower down, there were two end-scrapers described as carinated. At Temmata-Dupka in the Isker valley there is said to be an industry with Font-Yves points. 'Gravettian' material is said to be abundant in Rumania, but its age and typology have not been accurately assessed.

It is difficult to give any general picture of the Upper Palaeolithic in the European part of the USSR. Soviet archaeologists have long been more interested in the palaeo-sociological implications of their important discoveries than in their chronology or typology, and they were only too ready to attribute Western affinities to their industries. But this Upper Palaeolithic is extremely rich, diversified and original. It seems certain that different cultures must have co-existed, and also that in most cases this Palaeolithic does not fit into the framework of the west European industries. Fairly recently, Rogachev published a general survey of the stratigraphy of the Kostienki–Borchevo group of sites, situated on the River Don, which enables us to form some idea of the evolution of this Russian Palaeolithic.

According to Boriskovsky, the deposit at Rodomychle in the Ukraine not far from Kiev, excavated by Shovkopliass, would come at the very beginning. In the same layer there are numerous Mousterian-type flints, and a great many implements of Upper Palaeolithic type.

The site at Molodova v on the banks of the Dniester has yielded a complex stratigraphy, with eleven layers of Upper Palaeolithic overlying the Mousterian. Layer 10 contains a bifacial tanged leaf-shaped point, and the implements are of large dimensions, with well-retouched blades, end-scrapers, burins, etc., and big backed bladelets. Layer 9 is not very different; layer 8 contains a shouldered point which is not however typical. Layer 7 also contains some shouldered points, reminiscent rather of the French Upper Magdalenian, and a rich supply of bone implements. It has been dated by Carbon[14] at 21,740 ± 320 BC. Just as layer 10 had been styled 'Solutrean' because of its leaf-shaped bifacial specimen, so

*Figure 65 Jermanovician.* 1,7, points slightly
bifacially retouched at the base;
6, bifacial point. *Kostienki I*, lower level.
2, borer; 3, small round scraper;
4, side-scraper; 5, bifacial triangular point.

has this layer 7 been because of the tanged points; but it has really
nothing to do with this industry. Its affinities would rather be with
the Perigordian. Layers 4, 5 and 6 have produced other industries,
none of them very closely related to the West. Layer 3, which has
been assimilated to the Magdalenian, is dated 11,740 ± 540 BC
and has produced an anthropomorphic statuette. There are mammoths among the fauna. In layer 2 the industry includes small
almost thumb-nail-shaped end-scrapers, and dates from 9,950 ±
230 BC. It has been correlated with the Upper Magdalenian, with
which it shows some similarities. Layer 1a, said to be Azilian,
contains numerous burins, which is not usually the case in the
Azilian. A harpoon with two rows of barbs (and even the suggestion
of a third row) has a perforated base, but is neither Magdalenian
nor Azilian in style. Its date is 8,640 ± 230 BC. Layer 1 has some
clearly thumb-nail-shaped end-scrapers, various kinds of burins,
small and pointed backed blades, and backed bladelets. Reindeer
feature persistently in the fauna, but the mammoth disappears
after layer 3. It is rather strange to see the reindeer persisting so
late. Taken as a whole, in spite of a vague Magdalenian flavour in
layers 2 and 3, these industries have little relationship with the West.

In the same region the site at Babin I has also produced a stratigraphy. The lower layer, often assimilated to the Aurignacian,
contains retouched blade end-scrapers, which are not specifically
Aurignacian, burins, and some small pieces reminiscent of the
Font-Yves or the Krems points. Layer 2, lying above, has been
called Solutrean because of some bifacial specimens, and layer 3
Magdalenian. At Voronovitsa I the lower layer likewise contains
bifacial pieces, and the upper layer, which is rich in burins and
various end-scrapers, has been called Magdalenian. As in the case
of Molodova V, there hardly seems to be any foundation for these
assimilations.

The site of Mezin in the Desna basin has produced a rich indus-

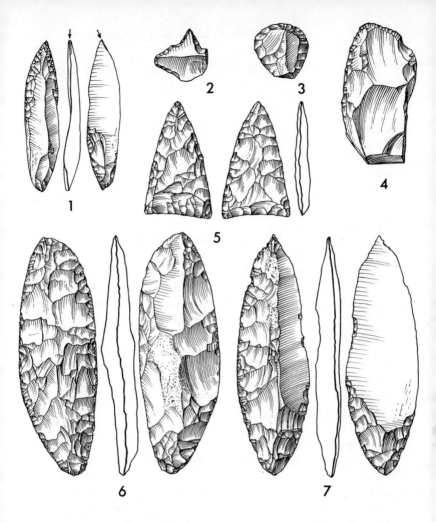

try of various kinds of burins, borers, end-scrapers, composite tools, truncated blades, backed blades, looking in general rather Magdalenian although burins on retouched truncation seem to be the dominant type. The bone implements include awls, a large needle or point with a perforated base decorated with slanting lines, and some grooved bone-points. There are numerous ornamental objects, and objects decorated with geometrical designs,

188

*Figure 66* Bone tools of the Russian Upper Palaeolithic. 1, broken implement, from Avdeyevo; 2, awl, same origin; 3, bone pin with pierced head, Kostienki iv, upper level; 4, 'shovel', Kostienki xv; 5, stylised swan (?), Malta; 6,7, objects from Malta.

some of which are probably stylised feminine forms. Bracelets have also been found with complex geometrical decorations, and bones decorated in the same way with red paint. There were also some traces of dwellings.

A little farther to the east, on the Seim, the site of Adveyevo has yielded an industry of the type produced by the upper layer of Kostienki i.

Thirty kilometres south of Voronezh on the River Don there is the Kostienki–Borchevo group, a complex of sites that vary in importance, situated in the colluvial loess. Some of them have produced a complicated stratigraphy. According to the recent work of Rogachev, the layers fall into three broad chronological stages, according to their situation with regard to the terraces, to the humic layers, and to a layer of volcanic ash.

1 *Old Upper Palaeolithic*: at the site known as Kostienki i, layer 5, the lowest of all, has produced an industry that has been wrongly labelled Solutrean. There are eleven flake end-scrapers, more or less fan-shaped, six burins (some transverse), four borers and some thin bifacial triangular points with a concave base (figure 65, 2,3,4,5) sometimes as much as five centimetres long but never thicker than five millimetres. There are two large rough laurel-leaves, a Mousterian point, several side-scrapers, thirty used flakes, and numerous unworked flakes; but hardly any blades, and what are found are of poor quality. The lower layer at Kostienki xii has produced some thick bifacial specimens, but no triangular ones. The latter recur in the one and only layer at Streletskaya ii. It is poor in implements (23 only), but has produced 4 of these triangular points. The Kostienki viii site (also known as Telmanskaya) (layer 4) has yielded a different industry, as has layer 2 at Kostienki xvii. The latter has produced in all nearly 10,000 flints, amongst which are twenty-two end-scrapers on blades or flakes, scrapers-burins, 150 burins, the majority of them on

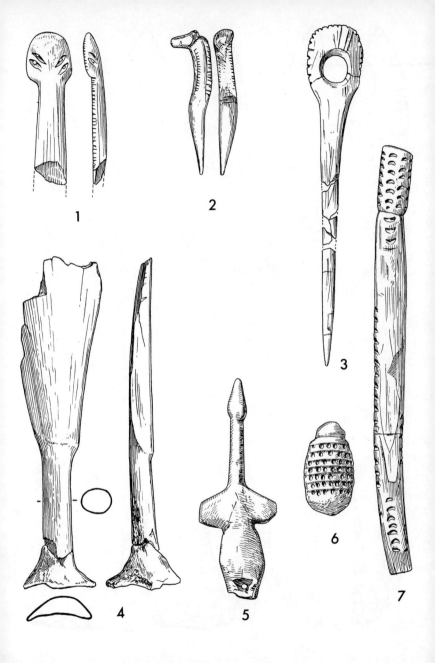

1  2  3  4  5  6  7

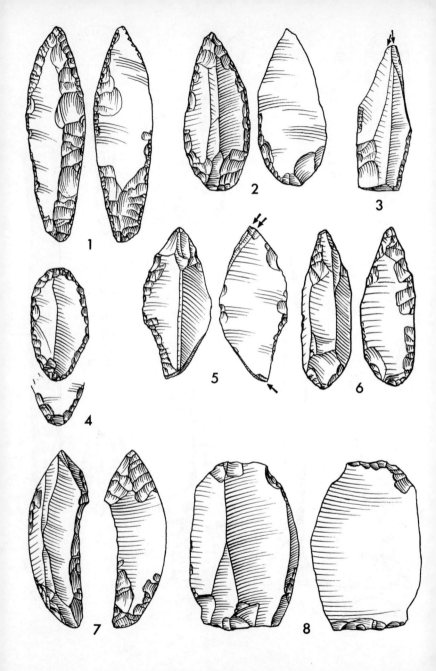

*Figure 67 Telmanskaya*, upper level.     191
1, Jermanovice point; 2, unifacial point; 3, burin;
4, end-scraper; 5, double burin. *Kostienki I*,
upper level. 6, Jermanovice point.
7, Kostienki-Willendorf point; 8, Kostienki knife.


retouched truncation, and often multiple; blades with worn edges,
two poor 'Kostienki knives'; a very occasional splintered piece; 110
retouched blades; hardly any backed pieces; fifteen cores, two
hammerstones, 1,800 flakes and about 7,000 small flakes. The bone
implements include two awls, two bone-point fragments and about
fifty pendants (canines of polar fox, fossil belemnites, shells and
pierced stones).

2 *Middle Upper Palaeolithic*. This is represented by various
levels; we shall only examine the chief ones. Layer 3 at the Telmanskaya site has produced six end-scrapers – one of them double –
nearly all on retouched blades. Burins are rare, and are sometimes
transverse and on a notch. There are retouched blades (one more
or less strangled) and several wands made of mammoth-tusk. Layer
2 has furnished about 6,000 flints, among which there are about 100
retouched blades, seventeen strongly retouched denticulate blades
and twenty-four finely retouched; at least five short end-scrapers,
seventy miscellaneous burins, some of them double opposed
dihedral burins; and more than 350 pointed backed blades, ninety-
three of them whole, either microgravettes or little bladelets with
both sides backed, but from the drawings it would be hard to say
whether they are backed bladelets or micro-Font-Yves. There are
also said to be six trapezoid implements (the one figured is reminiscent of a small Hamburgian point) and some triangles.

At Kostienki XII, the upper level has yielded different results at
different excavation-points. Point A has produced an industry with
end-scrapers on retouched blades, or short fan-shaped end-
scrapers, retouched blades, side-scrapers, and a little triangular
bifacial point. Point B has produced an industry akin to that at
Kostienki XV. This last site (also called Gorodtsovskaya, has
short end-scrapers, sometimes fan-shaped, retouched blades, sometimes pointed, borers, and about a dozen implements in the
Mousterian tradition. There are some bone 'shovels' (see figure

*Figure 68 Kostienki IV*, lower level. 1, denticulated backed bladelet; 2, 3, gravette points; 4, microgravette; 5, backed bladelet; 6, 7, scrapers; 8, 10, burins; 9, splintered piece.

66, 4), and some awls. Kostienki xiv (Markina Gora), layer 3, has yielded mainly burins and end-scrapers; and in layer 2 above, an industry that is strangely archaic-looking, with triangular unifacial points, discoid implements, miscellaneous side-scrapers, a few splintered pieces, some end-scrapers, no burins, and some bone awls.

3 *Evolved Upper Palaeolithic*. This is well represented by a variety of industries:

Layer 3 of Kostienki i seems to show some affinities with the Aurignacian, and so does layer 2. Layer 1 is the classical layer in this deposit. It includes a long dwelling-site 35 by 15 metres, with nine hearths in a line. The industry (figure 67, 6, 7, 8) comprises fine blades, sometimes retouched, 'Kostienki knives' (blades with inverse simple or double truncation and lateral retouching), Kostienki–Willendorf points (rather special tanged points with a broad blade) and Jermanovice points. There are also pointed reminiscent of those in Kostienki v; some double opposed dihedral burins, sometimes on a retouched blade, in which case they are reminiscent of those in Kostienki iv; some double opposed dihedral burins, which may be polyhedric, burins on retouched truncation, scrapers at the end of long or short blades, fan-shaped or almost thumb-nail-shaped scrapers, burin-scrapers, splintered pieces, discs, etc. The bone industry includes 'wedges', sometimes decorated with geometrical designs, long bone-points, curious sticks bulbous at one end, pierced sticks, spatulas or smoothing-tools, sometimes with enlarged and decorated heads, some human female statuettes and some animal ones.

The upper layer at the Telmanskaya site (figure 67, 1 to 5) is older, and would fit in chronologically between layers 2 and 3 of Kostienki i. It has produced Levallois flakes, Mousterian-type side-scrapers, often convergent or lopsided, Mousterian points bifacially retouched on their distal ends, some Jermanovice-type

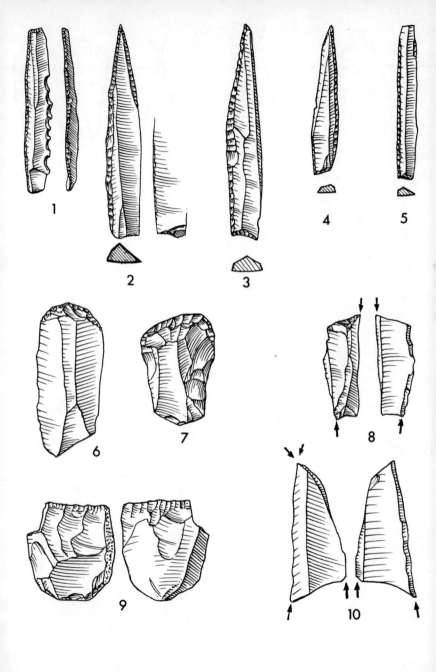

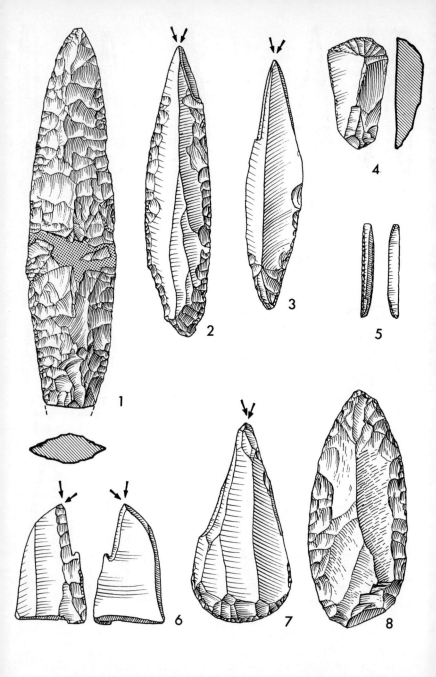

*Figure 69  Kostienki IV*, upper level.                                    195
1, bifacial point; 2, 3, long dihedral burins
on retouched blades; 4, end-scraper;
5, backed bladelet; 6, burin;
7, burin-scraper; 8, side-scraper.

points, leaf-shaped and almost entirely bifacial implements, true
plane-faced points rather like the Solutrean, but retouched in a
different way. Certain of these pieces show a clear tendency to
becoming tanged. There are also non-pointed leaf-shaped implements, burins (sometimes on broken points), dihedral burins
(sometimes double-ended), burins on retouched truncations, side-
scrapers, discs, small bifacial tools, awls and other bone implements. Taken as a whole, it looks a little archaic, although it
belongs to the upper series.

Kostienki II has produced the remains of a big oval dwelling
extending over 150 square metres, and built of mammoth-bones,
with a hearth in the centre and a burial-place at the side, also
surrounded by mammoth-bones, and a skeleton in a sitting posture. The industry comprises a large number of splintered pieces,
burins (often multiple), others dihedral or on truncation, scraper-
burins, scrapers on blade-ends, delicately retouched blades, and
bone awls (or perhaps cylindro-conical bone-points).

There are two important sites on the lower terrace of the Don.
Kostienki IV (Alexandrovskaya) has two layers, the lower one
producing good Gravette points, often fairly small, but sometimes
reaching a length of nine centimetres; large backed bladelets,
truncated or bitruncated into long rectangles, backed denticulate
bladelets, recalling those at Dolni Vestonice; burins, end-scrapers,
splintered pieces, and bone awls. This industry could without too
much difficulty be brought within the Upper Perigordian (see
figure 68). The upper layer has often been wrongly called Solutrean. It includes skilfully retouched blades, pointed backed
bladelets, fine dihedral straight burins on retouched blades, with a
pointed end opposite to the burin, exactly like some of the French
Protomagdalenian; dihedral double-opposed burins, burins on
truncation, scraper-burins, single or double end-scrapers, a fine
slender point with bifacial retouching, not in the least Solutrean,

and other bifacial pieces; a small shouldered and bifacially retouched point, Mousterian-looking side-scrapers, pierced discs
made from flat pebbles, partially polished implements made of
stone (not flint), partially polished pebbles; ivory points, awls with
natural heads or no heads, smoothing-tools notched at the side, a
strange large pin with a round head pierced with a hole, etc. In
spite of some resemblances with the Protomagdalenian at Laugerie-
Haute, the distance and the presence of certain characteristics
make convergence for the time being the only tenable hypothesis.
But there are also clear Western affinities in this upper layer (see
figure 69).

The site at Borchevo II is probably a good deal later. The lower
layer contains implements of small size: short end-scrapers, backed
bladelets and Azilian points. Burins are plentiful, especially those
on truncation. There are remains of mammoth among the fauna.
The middle layer has produced blades with worn edges, about forty
end-scrapers tending towards the thumb-nail-shaped type, about
seventy burins on truncation (sometimes multiple), dihedral burins,
and about twenty backed bladelets, together with about thirty that
have been very delicately retouched on one or two edges. In the
upper layer the industry is likewise small; and among the backed
pieces there are some entirely typical Azilian points. The reindeer
is present, but the mammoth has disappeared.

To the north of the Kostienki region, the deposit at Gargarino
has yielded numerous human statuettes and the remains of
dwellings.

In the Rostov region on the lower Don there is, according to
Boriskovsky, a special zone containing the seasonal encampments of men who hunted the great *bovidae*. Mention may be made
of the sites at Kamennaya Balka I and II, with small and sometimes thumb-nail-shaped end-scrapers, Azilian points with truncated base, and some pieces tending to become geometrical.

In the Crimea the lower layer of the deposit at Siuren I, in a rock shelter near Bakhchisarai, has produced an industry with high carinated scrapers like some that are found in Palestine; end-scrapers on large retouched blades, burins, points reminiscent of the Font-Yves, Dufour bladelets (sometimes truncated), and Mousterian-style implements which subsequently disappear. The middle layer has high carinated specimens, smaller quantities of Dufour bladelets, micro-Font-Yves, etc. The upper layer contains burins (dihedral ones in particular), end-scrapers, a few carinated pieces, a point suggesting a gravette (if the back is really steep), some backed bladelets – at least one of which is denticulate – some lunates and rather big rectangles. The site of Siuren II, close by, has given small end-scrapers, triangles, lunates, and (surprisingly enough) some points with retouching at the tip and the end, reminiscent of the Polish Masovian (figure 74, 6). Is this perhaps a convergence? At all events, this industry would appear to be a late one.

North-east of Moscow, the site of Sounghir near Vladimir has yielded an industry strikingly similar to that of Kostienki I layer 5 and Streletskaya II. It includes bifacial triangular points with concave bases, perhaps rather more evolved than at the other sites. There is a clear preponderance of flake-tools, with side-scrapers, some end-scrapers and some burins. Although distinctly more recent than Kostienki I, this site is perhaps older than the date of 12,000 before our era which has been suggested for it. There also exists a strongly stylised sculpture of a horse.

# 15 The Upper Palaeolithic in Asia

With the exception of the Middle East and Siberia, Asia is more or less unknown ground as far as the Upper Palaeolithic is concerned. One of the reasons for this is that, far more than in Europe, this Upper Palaeolithic industry continues the tradition of the Middle Palaeolithic; and failing any radio-carbon or geological dating, it is often difficult to say whether we are dealing with the former or the latter.

In Turkey, the Upper Palaeolithic is firmly linked with that of Palestine. It has been recognised at various sites, particularly in Southern Anatolia, on the Mediterranean coast (sites at Beldibi and Belbasi). The same is probably true for Iran. In Afghanistan, Coon's excavations at Kara Kamar, fourteen kilometres to the north of Haiback, are said to have unearthed in one layer an industry with 'Aurignacoïd' elements dated by Carbon[14] at probably 34,000 ± 3,000 before our time (32,000 BC).

In Iraq, the Zarzi cave, excavated by Garrod, contained a layer B 1·50 metres thick in places but thought to represent a single industry. It included little round end-scrapers, backed blades, and bladelets with strongly notched edges (small strangled blades). At the top there were geometric microliths, lunates, elongated triangles, and a single micro-burin. In the Pelagrawa cave (excavated by B. Howe) there was an analogous industry at the bottom. In the Shanidar cave, Iraqi Kurdistan, Solecki found two layers belonging to the Upper Palaeolithic above the Mousterian. Layer B (1·50 metres thick in places) contains an industry similar to that found at Zarzi. The approximate date given by radio-carbon dating for the bottom of the layer was 10,000 years BC. Layer C (three to four metres thick) contains an industry that has been named Baradostian. The top of the layer gave a date of about 27,000, the base about 33,000 BC. The industry – if there is indeed only one industry over the whole three metres of depth – contains numerous burins, sometimes on retouched blades, in which case they remind one of those in Kostienki IV or the Protomagdalenian, without of course any evident relationship; end-scrapers, some of them perhaps carinated, borers, retouched blades, Aurignacian-type strangled blades, and some used bones.

The Lebanon possesses some important sites, particularly at Ksar' Akil, the findings from which have not yet been made public. Here, over some twenty metres in thickness, there is a Mousterian industry and a whole series of Upper Palaeolithic layers super-imposed upon one another. In Syria as in Israel there are a large number of sites. Neuville – followed by Garrod – has divided this Upper Palaeolithic into six stages. Phase I is said to be a transitional industry, where blades and blade-tools are associated with a high proportion of points and side-scrapers of Mousterian type. There were said to be backed knives and end-scrapers on unretouched blades. The burins were not typical. The typical implement, 'though always rare', was the Emireh point, an unretouched Levallois point, with the base thinned by bifacial retouching. Phase II, which was ill-defined, is only known from a few deposits. In the course of phase III, there is a falling off in the number of Mousterian forms and the Aurignacian ones begin to appear. There are small retouched blades said to be Font-Yves points, although more often than not they are more pointed than these. There is an abundance of carinated end-scrapers. In phase IV, Font-Yves became rare, the Aurignacian characteristics became more definite, and nose-scrapers appear, as well as not very typical busked burins. Backed knives are very rare, in fact most of them being only obliquely truncated blades. The bone implements in phases III and IV do not amount to more than a few biconical points. Garrod suggests as a name for these phases Lower and Upper Antelian. Phase V – the Atlitian – is rather rare and enigmatical. At El Wad, Mount Carmel, eighty per cent of the implements consist of carinated end-scrapers and 'prismatic burins' (narrow

*Figure 70* Upper Palaeolithic
from Siberia. Ust' Kanskaya Cave.
1, burin; 2, bifacial point;
3, retouched blade; 4, borer;
5, chopping-tool; 6, Mousterian point.

carinate). Phase VI (the Kebaran) has attenuated Aurignacian characteristics, and a profusion of backed bladelets, sometimes pointed at both ends.

Thanks to the kindness of Rust and Waechter, I have been able to view all the material from Jabrud (Syria) and part of that from Ksar'Akil. Certain levels in these deposits are so close to the French Aurignacian, in spite of some inevitable minor differences, not only in the individual typology of specimens but even in their proportions, that it may be questioned whether a separate name for them is desirable. Layer 10 at Ksar'Akil in particular is definitely Aurignacian. It is earlier than $26,500 \pm 380$ BC – the date of layer 8. Before these Aurignacian levels come layers whose industries do not seem to run altogether in the Aurignacian direction. Layer 16 for example contains blades with a thin curved back, and plane-faced points in the Solutrean style – another example of convergence (figure 74, 8). After the Aurignacian layers the evolution takes a rather unexpected direction, and layer 6, to judge from the few square metres examined, looks like Lower Magdalenian, which poses the problem of convergence not for a single type but for whole industrial complexes.

There is, too, another problem at Jabrud, the problem of layer 15, which has been styled 'Pre-Aurignacian'. This industry already has stongly-marked Upper Palaeolithic characteristics, but probably dates from the end of Würm II and lies beneath fourteen layers of evolved Mousterian in which burins in particular develop. The old date proposed by Rust and Garrod (Last Interglacial) is hardly tenable today. What happened to this Pre-Aurignacian? Was it an abortive attempt, or was it the true ancestor of an Upper Palaeolithic industry?

Practically nothing is known about the Upper Palaeolithic in India or Malaysia. In China, there is an Upper Palaeolithic industry in the upper cave at Choukoutien. It has produced five thin layers

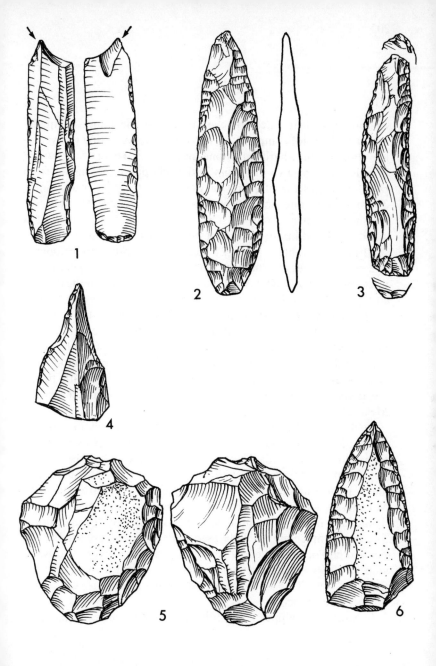

without any clear traces of evolution, and the fauna is equally uniform. The stone implements are very few, consisting of twenty-five tools of flint, hard sandstone and quartz. There are a variety of side-scrapers, two choppers and a chopping-tool made from pebbles, and a series of quartz flakes made by the bipolar technique. There is only one bone implement – an eyed needle; and two polished fragments, one of a stag's antler and the other of a mandible. In addition: seven limestone beads adhering to a human skull in a burial-place, and 125 pierced teeth, probably belonging to a necklace. Other ornamental objects were a pierced pebble and three pierced sea-shells. All these objects are a clear indication of an Upper Palaeolithic stage, for which there might have been some doubt in view of the stone industry. This was probably a burial-cave rather than a dwelling-place. The Upper Palaeolithic here is rather late; because of the needle and the pierced teeth, it has been compared to that at Afontava Gora in Siberia. The skeletons that have been found are of the modern type, tall, and with mixed racial characteristics, some Caucasoid, others Mongoloid or even Melanesian.

In the Ordos desert, on the Sjara-osso-gol, a tributary of the Huang-Ho, there is an Upper Palaeolithic site which was excavated long ago by Teilhard. There is no local raw material, and the implements are therefore small. The fauna is rich, but the implements poor (only about two hundred pieces). There are very small Mousterian-looking side-scrapers or points, short end-scrapers, denticulate implements, little pebble choppers and definite burins. The bone implements include used bone splinters, polished at the pointed end or retouched by percussion; and the tip of a flat wand with two convergent incisions, which was found a short distance from the site. This industry would seem older than that in the upper Choukoutien cave.

In Siberia the Upper Palaeolithic presents a number of different facies. In the hills of the western Altaï the Ust' Kanskaya cave (see figure 70) produces Mousterian-tradition implements, with Levalloisian flakes, poor quality bifacial tools, discs, side-scrapers, massive blades, and points in the Mousterian style; but also some borers, one or two burins, and a fine leaf-shaped bifacial implement polished by use; some used bone splinters, one or two bone pendants, and a notched bone.

There is a site at Malta, on the left bank of the Belava in the Lake Baikal region, 85 kilometres west of Irkutsk. It has produced several dwellings, and an original industry, comprising end-scrapers, side-scrapers, borers and retouched blades – one of which still had its deer-antler handle – some burins, notched pieces, bone needles and awls, and some points. Works of art were also numerous, among them female statuettes, statuettes representing stylised swans (?), and the drawing of a mammoth. At Buriet, on the right bank of the Angora, there were four dwellings yielding an industry reminiscent of that at Malta, and also two female statuettes.

These two sites no doubt belong to an advanced Upper Palaeolithic. The site of Afontava Gora on the Yenissei is probably later, and typologically more akin to Ust' Kanskaya. There were bifacial tools, discs, side-scrapers, Mousterian points, large and small end-scrapers, retouched blades, small backed bladelets, and microlithic points. The bone implements included needles and awls, and grooved points. Among the ornamental objects were some pierced teeth.

# 16 The Upper Palaeolithic in Africa

It is very difficult to define the Upper Palaeolithic in Africa except from the chronological point of view; and even this aspect of it is far from easy. For in this way one would have to introduce Mousteroid forms at the bottom, and would have to exclude the Capsian at the top, as being almost entirely post-glacial, although of all the African industries it is the most like the classic Upper Palaeolithic.

In North Africa, following on from the Mousterian and no doubt derived from it, is an industry that is certainly Upper Palaeolithic in spite of its old name of 'Tanged Mousterian'. This is Aterian. The basic types of implements are certainly still Mousterian, as shown by the often very true use of the Levallois technique and by the numerous side-scrapers, points, etc. But there are also a good number of end-scrapers and gravers, and the distribution of types is quite different from that of the Mousterian. The original feature is the development of tanged implements (see figure 71, 2), of which the points only constitute one aspect. As Tixier justly observes, the Aterians added tangs to almost everything, including flakes. Tanged artifacts already appear in sporadic fashion in the North African Mousterian.

Balout distinguishes three evolutionary stages in Aterian – Old Aterian, along the coast; then Middle or Classical Aterian; and lastly Final Aterian, only found in Morocco and the Sahara. This last stage developed leaf-shaped points with bifacial retouch and tanged points with bifacial retouch (figure 71, 1,5). It was these bifacial leaf-shaped pieces that were responsible for the very unlikely hypothesis of an African origin for Solutrean.

The Aterian is met with as far afield as the Kharga oasis in Egypt, and in an evolved form on the northern borders of the ancient Lake Chad.

For a long time the only African industry apparently deserving the name of Upper Palaeolithic seemed to be the typical Capsian of

Tunisia, which certain typological convergences caused to be compared with Perigordian (Old or Upper Aurignacian, as it was then called). But it came to be realised that this Capsian is very late, and at the most contemporary in its older forms with the Upper Magdalenian. The Capsian zone lies in the interior of Tunisia, in the Gafsa region. The deposits consist of shell middens or ash-heaps (rammadiya) composed of ashes, burnt stones, snail-shells, chipped flints and animal bones. The implements comprise numerous backed blades, often large in size and in higher proportions than in the Perigordian; large denticulate or strangulated blades, numerous burins, especially on truncation; various end-scrapers in smaller numbers, a high percentage of backed bladelets, triangles, lunates, and microburins which are waste pieces from the making of the microliths (figure 71, 3,4,6 to 12). The bone industry includes in particular some tapering awls, perhaps used as snail-needles. It is certain that the relationships between Capsian and Perigordian are extremely distant, assuming they actually do exist.

Ibero-Maurusian is a different industry, whose clumsy name goes back to a time when it was thought to extend over both the Maghreb and Spain. It is characterised by an overwhelming proportion of backed bladelets, with few end-scrapers or flint geometric forms and only rare burins. This industry is much more widespread than the typical Capsian, and seems to be linked with the Mechta-el-Arbi race, a North African variant of the Cro-Magnon people.

In Tunisia there is an older industry in the Gafsa region, in the silts overlying the high terrace at Sidi Mansour and Lala. It contains numerous backed bladelets and end-scrapers, but no burins or microburins. This might well be an ancestor of the Ibero-Maurusian.

In Cyrenaica, McBurney's excavations at Hagfet ed Dabba and Haua Fteah have unearthed industries which might go back at the

*Figure 71 Aterian.* 2, tanged point, el Djouf, Algeria.
*Evolved Aterian.* 1, bifacial tanged point, Tit Mellil,
Morocco; 5, bifacial point, same origin. *Capsian.*
3,4,7, trapezes; 6, denticulated blade; 8, burin; 9, small
triangle; 10, end-scraper; 11, lunate; 12, backed blade.

oldest to about 30,000 years. This Dabban industry with its backed blades, gravers and end-scrapers has been compared to the Middle East Emiran, by virtue of the existence in both industries of transverse burins, though these are found in many other cultures.

In Egypt, E. Vignard's researches long ago produced evidence for the existence of the Sebilian industry, derived from a Mousterian with Levalloisian flakes, and characterised by Levallois flakes with truncated base. Evolved Sebilian contains microliths.

Sebilian II has recently been dated at about 11,000 BC. Recent research by Philip Smith in the same Kom Ombo region where Vignard had found Sebilian has led to fresh discoveries. Kom Ombo lies on the eastern bank of the Nile, about fifty kilometres north of Aswan. Near Djebel Silsileh, Smith found two new industries lying in stratigraphical order. The Silsilan dates from 13,360 ± 200 BC and contains microburins, backed bladelets, burins, some geometric flints, etc. Sebekian, which overlies it, is clearly different. There are no microburins or geometric flints; but there are long narrow blades delicately retouched towards the base, bladelets of the same type, good quality burins, end-scrapers and side-scrapers. The age is about 12,000 to 13,000 BC. These two industries would seem to be related to the old Ibero-Maurusian as represented at Lala or Sidi Mansour in Tunisia.

South of the Sahara, the 'Middle Stone Age' seems to correspond more or less with the Upper Palaeolithic. In the Congo forests and in Angola, Lupemban is derived from Sangoan, and comes in to takes its place. Early Lupemban still contains a good number of Sangoan forms (such as picks and occasional bifacial tools); but its implements are generally smaller and better fashioned. There are chisels, adzes, boat-shaped planes, a quantity of side-scrapers, and blades, some of them having chamfered backs. The most characteristic tool is the lanceolate bifacial point (see figure 44). Upper Lupemban contains the same types, but more delicately

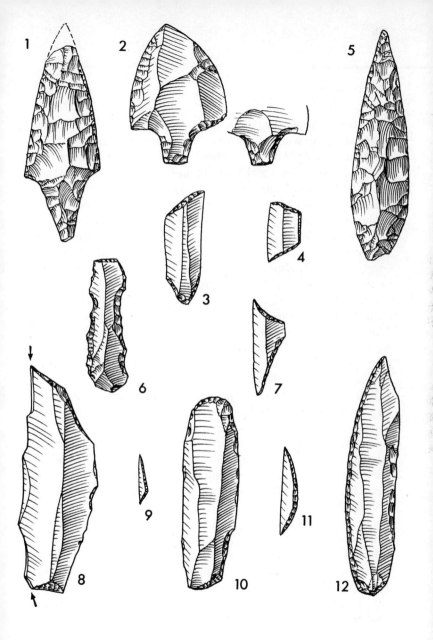

retouched; backed blades develop, and the leaf-shaped points sometimes have wavy edges. Sometimes there are tanged points. At the Mufo site in Angola, Carbon[14] dating has given a figure of about 12,500 BC for Final Lupemban. In northern Angola tanged points and backed blades are later in appearing (figure 44, 4).

In Zambia and Malawe the Lupemban crops up again with most of the implements typical of this industry.

In southern South Africa there are two distinct and contemporary industries along the coast. To the west, and running right along the coast through the dunes, is the Stillbay culture; but it is also found in the Skildergat cave. Apart from the typical side-scrapers, it contains backed blades, more or less slender and well-worked leaf-shaped bifacial tools, and unifacial points with denticulate edges. This classical Stillbay no doubt includes several stages. Farther east we meet with the Mossel-Bay culture in the Cape of Saint Blaize cave and at other places. The characteristic implement is a sort of Levallois point with little or no retouching.

In Zambia and Rhodesia the Stillbay series begins with Rhodesian Proto-Stillbay, containing unifacial points, side-scrapers, some handaxes and occasionally some thick bifacial points. It is in association with an industry of this type that the Neanderthaloid man was found, at Broken Hill in Zambia. This Proto-Stillbay passes over into Rhodesian Stillbay during the second half of the Gamblian period. The implements are the same in type but better fashioned, and include some leaf-shaped bifacial tools. In the Bambata cave, southern Rhodesia, Stillbay contains some large lunates, and perhaps some burins.

In the Transvaal we meet with the so-called Pietersburg industry, sometimes found in caves or shelters, but often in open-air sites. This Pietersburgian is rather similar to southern Rhodesian Still-bay. It can be divided into three or four stages, and it probably evolves towards Magosian. Beyond the Vaal in the Orange Free

State there are other imperfectly known forms, amongst which is the 'Hagenstadt variant'. Contemporary with the Middle Pieters-burgian, the Mazelspoort variant (near Bloemfontein) is probably responsible for the Rose Cottage Cave Magosian at Ladybrand. In Western Griqualand the Alexandersfontein variant, south of Kimberley, appears in two stages, the older with handaxes like those in the Fauresmith, the more recent with elongated points.

In the eastern region, the industries from the southern part seem to be more related to the Mazelspoort and Alexandersfontein variants, whilst in north-western Natal and Swaziland they are nearer to the Pietersburgian, but of a rather special type with fine elongated leaf-shaped points.

# 17 Japan, various islands and Australia

There is no longer any debate, as there was some years ago, as to the existence of Palaeolithic in Japan; but its age is still far from certain. To judge from the fauna, Japan was attached to the continent during a good part of the Pleistocene period; and it is therefore perfectly possible, as Choukoutien fauna is present, that man arrived at the same time. But at present there is no absolute proof of this. In the north-east of Kyushu island, two sites have been ascribed to Lower Palaeolithic. At Nyu there is an industry with choppers, chopping-tools and even one or two handaxes which has been attributed to a yellowish layer topped by a red soil said to be interglacial; but it would seem that only one flake has been found for certain *in situ*. This industry may very well belong to the old Asiatic Palaeolithic or be later. At Sozudai the age is likewise uncertain and the industry a matter of debate. There may also perhaps be some industries at the beginning of the Würm, but the majority of the sites do not at present appear to be older than 20 to 25,000 years. There are mammoth remains in Hokkaido island and the Ordos fauna in the rest of Japan.

In Hokkaido there is a blade industry, particularly of obsidian rather than flint, dated by $C^{14}$ and obsidian hydration measurements to between 18,000 and 6,000 BC, according to the sites. It contains burins and a variety of scrapers, as well as 'Shirataki burins' on cores, which are perhaps no more than blade-cores. These cores have the peculiarity of being first of all worked into large bifacial tools. In addition, it includes points and bifacial knives.

Smaller blades with steeply chamfered backs are found in the Tokio region and farther west; but flat bifacial retouched points are also present in this region. These bifacial points are generally thought to be more recent than the backed blades, but their exact relationship is not known with any certainty. Sometimes there are also microlithic forms.

The site at Iwajaku in the Kanto plain (Hondo or Honshu island) has produced in its lower layer an industry with big blades and bifacial tools. One of these bifacial tools shows signs of having been polished on the edge, but it is older than 11,180 BC. This part-polishing crops up in other Japanese Palaeolithic sites. The site of Gongenyama – also in the northern part of the Kanto plain – has yielded curiously Acheulean-looking handaxes and some flake-tools.

There is no doubt at all that Palaeolithic studies are now greatly developing in Japan.

The islands lying between Japan and Java have produced Palaeolithic remains; but these are often at present impossible to date. Moreover, given the conservatism of the Asiatic Palaeolithic, they might equally well belong to the equivalent of Upper, Middle, or even Lower Palaeolithic. At Luzon in the northern Philippines, Von Koenigswald has reported finding pebble tools looking like Acheulean handaxes with only one worked face, the other being formed by the natural convex surface of the pebble. This procedure was often used by the Acheuleans; but at present there is nothing to indicate the age of this industry. In the southern Celebes, Von Heekeren has likewise reported a flake-industry at Tjabengé which has been attributed to layers with dwarf *Archidiskodon* (elephant), but which appears to have been found on the surface in association with the fauna. There were sixty-seven implements in all, with side-scrapers and some rough blades. The whole would date from the Pleistocene, and has been compared with the Upper Palaeolithic assemblage of Sangiran in Java.

In Borneo the findings are more precise. The Niah cave in Sarawak is an enormous cavity about 240 metres broad and 60 metres high at its mouth. The soundings that have been published did not go below 3·60 metres. The superficial layers contain remains of the Iron Age, the Bronze Age, and Late and Early

Mesolithic. The Palaeolithic deposits begin between 1 and 1·5 metres below the top surface. A level between 1·05 and 1·80 metres gave dates of about 18,000 and 30,000 BC; and at the bottom were pebble-tools and large flakes, becoming smaller going up the section. The whole has been compared to the Upper Soan in India. At about 2·50 metres – dated at 38,000 BC – near a human skull a single flake was found which reminded Paterson very strongly of the Middle Soan flakes in India. It is perhaps rash to venture to draw conclusions from a single flake! The human skull is said to be modern in type; and if the date is accurate, this would be one of the most ancient known to us.

Until quite recently Australia was considered to be a continent populated at a very late period; but new discoveries are tending to throw doubts upon this point of view. A date of about 17,000 BC has been arrived at for the site at Lake Menindee in New South Wales, where there is a layer containing a hearth and a flake. For an industry containing a chopper in the Noola shelter, also in New South Wales, a date of about 9,600 BC has been obtained. In Kenniff Cave, Queensland, at a depth of 2·15 metres, a date of about 9,000 BC has been arrived at, and there is still one metre of deposits below this. It is therefore certain that Australia was populated in Palaeolithic times – in the chronological sense – since the Palaeolithic in the cultural sense was still going on there not long ago.

# 18 The Palaeolithic in America

The idea that there could be a Palaeolithic stage in America associated with extinct forms of animal life was not accepted without considerable opposition. This opposition sometimes took on ridiculous forms, as for example when the great anthropologist Hrdlicka refused to admit that the various human fossils discovered were at all old on the pretext that they belonged to the 'modern' type! From this point of view, Chancelade or Cro-Magnon man would not have found favour in his sight. This cautious outlook meant that the early discoveries were hedged about with a superabundance of qualifications. When the first Folsom point was discovered in New Mexico in 1926, in association with a bison of extinct species, three expeditions and the discovery of several points *in situ* among the bone-remains were required to produce conviction in the anthropologists. Yet there was nothing of an *a priori* nature against the existence of Palaeolithic men in America.

Moreover, as almost everywhere else outside the classical European zone, the concept of Palaeolithic man is difficult to define. A large part of the American sites date from the post-glacial, but are found side by side with a fauna which had long been extinct in Europe; and they belong to a definitely Palaeolithic cultural stage, without agriculture or pottery or domestic animals. But it now seems certain that the arrival of man took place during the Palaeolithic period, and before the post-glacial.

Since America is a continent, it would be difficult to make even a summary study of it in a few pages. Moreover, American Palaeolithic prehistory is a complicated subject about which little is at present known. Few dwelling-sites have been explored, and few results published. The majority of them are 'kill sites', where there are only a few implements lying around that have been used for killing and cutting up the carcases of one or more animals.

Certain authors allow that there was a stage without projectile points, when only a crude industry existed. For this stage Carbon[14]

*Figure 72* Palaeo-Indian implements from America. 1, Clovis point; 2, Sandia point; 3, Folsom point; 4, Fell's Cave point; 5, scraper; 6, knife or side-scraper; 7, projectile point. (4 to 7, Fell's Cave.)

dates have been proposed ranging sometimes as far back as 26 or 36,000 BC. Unfortunately the relationship is by no means clear between the implements and the burnt wood or bones that served to date them. Although man may possibly have invaded America in the remote past, there is not at present any absolute proof of this. And a date of 36,000 BC would, as we shall see, be surprising.

On the other hand the Palaeo-Indian stage is now clearly established. At present there are no certain dates going further back than 7,000 to 8,000 BC, which would make the cultures contemporary with our Mesolithic. But these cultures are already sufficiently diversified to suggest the presence of man for some thousands of years, and dates of the order of 10 to 15,000 BC would not be at all unreasonable.

The Sandia cave in New Mexico has yielded projectile points of a particular type beneath a level containing Folsom points. These Sandia points are bifacial, and have a slight shoulder (figure 72, 2). Together with them were side-scrapers, flakes, etc. This stratigraphy would be of the first importance, but there has recently been some criticism of the excavating technique.

At Lucy (New Mexico) Sandia points have been found, some of them fluted, along with mammoth remains, bifacially retouched tools and a tanged end-scraper of a type known also in Asia. Some Sandia points and a tanged end-scraper have also been discovered in Alberta, Canada.

The next (or perhaps contemporary) industry seems to be of the type called Clovis, found at Blackwater Draw between Clovis and Portales in New Mexico. The men responsible for this culture seem to have hunted the mammoth, for at various sites these points have been discovered in association with the bones of this animal. These Clovis points are lanceolate, with slightly concave base, worked by percussion and thinned down along their axis by the more or less successful removal of a small blade on each face (i.e. fluted points;

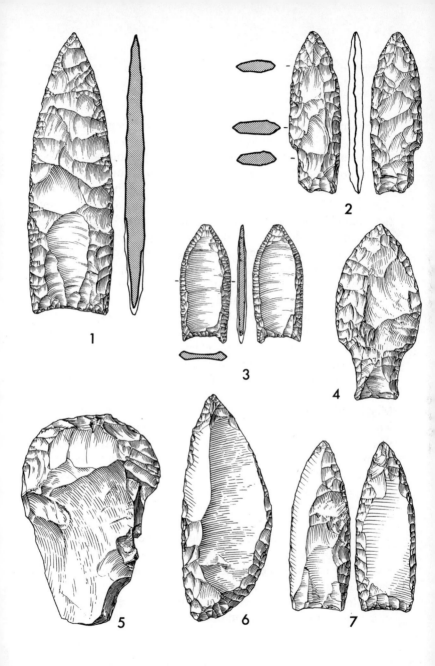

see figure 72, 1). In the case of the Clovis points, which are relatively thick, this removal can be effected by percussion. This is at present an absolutely unknown technique outside the New World, and might well rank as the first American patent. Along with these flint points were two bone points with bevelled bases. Above the Clovis point level came a level producing Folsom points (see figure 72, 3). These are likewise 'fluted' points, but lighter, more squat, and more delicately worked, mostly by pressure. The grooves seem to have been made – according to the experimental work carried out by Crabtree – either by indirect percussion or by pectoral pressure. The most important site is at Lindenmeier in New Mexico; it was excavated between 1934 and 1938, but the results have unfortunately not yet been published. As well as fluted points, this industry contains the same type of point, but without fluting; leaf-shaped knives with bifacial retouching, some of which remind one of the Solutrean laurel-leaves; small short end-scrapers on retouched blades or flakes, often formed with a projecting spur as the edge; 'becs' or borers reminiscent of those in the Lower Magdalenian, side-scrapers – sometimes concave – and even (from what we have seen) some burins. Some choppers, hammer stones, some grinding stones (sometimes colour-stained), blocks of haematite and flakes. A haematite bead, one of lignite and tubular bone beads constituted the ornaments. There were also some bone awls, perhaps some bone-points, and three bone discs decorated with incisions round their circumference. At various places this Folsom culture has given Carbon[14] dates of about 8,000 BC. The Folsom men were especially hunters of the bison.

The site of the Hell Gap in Wyoming, which is at present being excavated, has produced an impressive stratigraphy which when published will certainly make it a key deposit.

In Mexico there have been finds of mammoth remains in association with projectile points and other implements dating from about

8,000 BC. It is interesting to note that about 8,000 to 7,000 BC man was already present in South Patagonia, in the Palli Aike and Fell's caves (see figure 72, 4 to 7).

This brief summary can only give a very imperfect idea of the complexity of the Palaeolithic and Epipalaeolithic industries in America. There are also some interesting questions on which it will be as well to say a few words concerning the peopling of the New World, and the convergences of its industries with those of the ancient world.

Many authors – even quite recently – have been struck with the resemblances between the Palaeo-Indian and the Solutrean points, and have wanted to interpret this in terms of contact or relationship. But this is clearly a difficult hypothesis to uphold. True, certain likenesses do indeed exist: some of the Spanish Solutrean points would be perfectly in place in the Clovis or Folsom industries, or in those which followed them. Both groups practised pressure-flaking as well as percussion. Again, the internal balance of the stone industry (numerous end-scrapers, numerous projectile-points and bifacial knives, well developed borers, infrequent burins, side-scrapers in the Middle Palaeolithic style, fairly rare bone industries) – all this presents certain resemblances. And these resemblances may sometimes even extend to details: for instance, we have found in the Laugerie-Haute Lower Solutrean a decorated ivory fragment reminiscent of the Lindenmeier discs. Since the hypothesis of a direct relationship must clearly be ruled out for obvious reasons, this is an excellent example of the length to which convergences can go. Another instance is provided by the El Inga industry near Quito in Equador, dated according to different authors from 7,000 to 3,000 BC. It contains a whole series of multiple burins on truncation, and burin-scrapers which would – apart from their raw material, obsidian – be absolutely in place in French Upper Perigordian.

But western Europe is of course not the place to look for the origin of the Palaeo-Indian cultures, for man certainly reached America by way of the Bering Straits, which were dry land during the glacial periods. Perhaps however the very severe climate meant that the passage was only possible during the Würmian inter-stadials. One of these dates from before 30,000 BC, and the other from about 14 to 15,000 years. If it is agreed that man arrived during this second period, that would fit in well with the absolute dates obtained for the Palaeo-Indian deposits much farther south. But the first possibility cannot be absolutely excluded, for it may be that the Bering Straits could be crossed by well-equipped men outside the interstadials, men who were used to Arctic conditions, as the men of the Upper Palaeolithic in Siberia may well have been. However this may be, the conquest by modern man of a virgin and habitable continent was an adventure unique in human history, unless perhaps one cites the case of Australia. There can be no repetition of this until man lands on a planet belonging to another star. Once man had reached Alaska, there was the problem of how to continue south when the route – except during the interstadials or the periods of glacier recession – was barred by ice. But one thing is certain: man found a way through.

The diversity of the Indian tribes no less than the diversity of Palaeo-Indian cultures suggest that there were several successive waves of advance. Were these true migrations, or simply the extension of hunting-grounds, a slow displacement of the territorial centre of gravity of various tribes? Perhaps it was both. Contrary to the opinion of Marie Wormington, we should hold that there have always been adventurous people seeking to find out what there was on the far side of the ranges. The emptiness of the American continent no doubt speeded this expansion. Once the regions of ice had been left behind, game must have been abundant and the population must have expanded rapidly, with an equally rapid loss of contact between the tribes, leading to cultural and even genetic drift, probably of an important kind. Eight or nine thousand years is not such a large span of time for the journey from Alaska to the Terra del Fuego, especially with the formidable barrier of the South American mountains and forests. It seems difficult to believe that the only process involved was the normal extension of hunting-grounds: the pushing forward towards new frontiers must surely also have played its part.

# 19 A general review of the Upper Palaeolithic period

The Upper Palaeolithic period saw a continuance of the gradual disintegration of the original cultural unity. And the diversity of its primitive stages, which began just a little later than the Mousterian, precludes the idea that the transition from one to the other occurred in just one place from which the Upper Palaeolithic then spread abroad. There must have been many points of transition, and many and varying origins. In western Europe, there is no difficulty in tracing back the origin of the Perigordian to the Mousterian of the Acheulean tradition. Now the human type of the Lower Perigordian, probably represented by the remains found at Combe-Capelle (Dordogne), was a man of modern type even if he showed some primitive characteristics. It is impossible to make him into an invader bringing with him a Lower Perigordian culture, for the very good reason that this culture is unknown outside western Europe. We should have to make this invader arrive with an industry perfectly adapted to follow the Mousterian of Acheulean-tradition, which would then conveniently disappear at that precise moment. It is much more probable that one is a descendant of the other. But the implications would then be either that Acheulean-tradition man was already modern in type – which is possible, since he is an unknown quantity – or that the physical evolution involved in the transition from Neanderthal to modern man partly took place in western Europe. Is this after all so impossible? Are we to suppose that some special curse rests upon Europe?

The Aurignacian, on the other hand, appears to come from elsewhere, though its origin is something of a mystery. From France to the Middle East there is a kind of trail of Aurignacian clues of a more or less definite sort suggesting that there must be some link between the ancient Aurignacian industries of East and West. But it must be recognised that at present it is not possible to have any very clear idea as to the origin of the Aurignacian, unless perhaps that it is derived from the Jabrud Pre-Aurignacian. We should probably look in the direction of a more or less Quina-type Mousterian. Emiran (or better, Emirehan), at least as far as the findings have been published, hardly seems to be a possible ancestor; for like the Early Perigordian, it contains both Mousterian and Upper Palaeolithic forms, but it does not seem to tend towards the Aurignacian. This is a point on which the publication of the results from Ksar'Akil will be most welcome. It may well be that the Middle East sequence is more complicated than had been supposed.

One thing is certain. The Aurignacian and the Perigordian are not derived from one another, nor from the same ancestor. In central Europe there is at least one other evolution. The Szeletian with its leaf-shaped specimens comes probably from the Mousterian with *Blattspitzen*. But what are its relationships with the Jermanovician in Poland? There are leaf-shaped pieces at Jermanovice and Jermanovician-type points with leaf-shaped specimens at Ranis in Germany. This industry is perhaps a pointer to certain Russian Upper Palaeolithic assemblages (Telmanskaya upper layer), but certainly not to the Perigordian or the Aurignacian. True, there are some Aurignacian types in the Hungarian Szeletian sites, and vice versa; but this should probably be taken rather as a sign that they were contemporary than traceable to a common origin.

In Russia the industry in the bottom layer of Kostienki I, representing one of the oldest manifestations of the Upper Palaeolithic in this region, has little in common with the Perigordian, the Aurignacian or even the Szeletian, in spite of the bifacial points – triangular here – and the two rough leaf-shaped points. Their origin should rather be sought in a Starocelie-Volgograd-type Mousterian. But Telmanskaya layer 4 differs. And if the lower layer of Kostienki XVII is really contemporary, this again is something different. These industries undergo evolution, and there are

*Figure 73* Chronological chart of the Upper Palaeolithic in Europe. In the column about Russia, some sites have two dates, one from $C^{14}$, the other one from Rogachev's stratigraphy.

| | C.14 | France (S.W) | | Belgium | Holland | Germany | Poland |
|---|---|---|---|---|---|---|---|
| Post-Würm | 9,100 | Mesolithic | | | | | |
| | | Azilian | | Tjonger group. (etc.) | Ahrensburgian Tjonger group. | Ahrensburgian (etc.) | Pludian |
| | 9,500 | | | | | | |
| Würm IV | | Magdalenian VI² Magdalenian VI¹ Magdalenian V | | Upper Magdalenian | Late palaeolithic (?) | Upper Magdal. Hamburgian | Masovian + Tarnovian |
| | | Magdalenian IV | | | | Hamburgian | Magdalenian |
| | 15,000 | Magdalenian III Magdalenian II Magdalenian I Magdalenian '0' | | | | | |
| Würm III/ Würm IV | 17,000 17,500 | Final Solutrean Upper Solutrean | | | | | |
| | | Middle Solutrean | | Final Upper Perigordian | | | |
| | 19,000 | Lower Solutrean | | | | | |
| | 20,000 | Perig. VII (Proto-Magdalenian) Perigordian VI Perigordian V | Aurignacian V | | | | |
| | 22,000 | Perigordian IV | | Perigordian V | | Upper Perigordian (?) | |
| Würm III | | | Aurignac. IV | | | | 'Perigordian' |
| | | Evolved | Aurignac. III | | | Evolved | |
| | 27,000 | Lower Perigordian | Aurignac. II | Aurignac. II (?) | | Aurignacian | |
| | 29,000 | | Aurignacian I | Aurignacian I | | Aurignacian I | Aurignacian Jermanovicia |
| Würm III/ Würm II | 32,000 33,000 | Lower Perigord. | Aurignacian '0' | | | Blattspitzen culture (?) | |
| | 36,000 | Final Mousterian? | | | | | Jermanovicia |
| Würm II | 37,000 | Mousterian | | Mousterian | | Mousterian | |

| Czechoslovakia (C) Austria (A) | Hungary | U.S.S.R. (Europe) | Spain W | Spain E | Italy |
|---|---|---|---|---|---|
| | | Molodova V (I.1a) | | | |
| | | | Azilian | Epipalaeolithic | Late Romanellian |
| Magdalenian | Magdalenian (?) | Molodova V (I.2) Siuren II Borchevo II Molodova V (I.3) Kostienki I, I.1 (C.14 date) Markina-Gora, I.3 (C.14) | Magdal. VI | Magdal. VI | Romanellian |
| | | Siuren I (?) | Magdal. III | Magdalenian I - II - III | |
| | 'Gravettian' | | Final Solutr. Upper Solutrean | Final Solutr. Upper Solutrean | |
| | | Kostienki XVII (C.14) Kostienki I, I.1 (expected date) | | | 'Evolved Perigordian' |
| | | | Middle Solutrean | Middle Solutrean (?) | |
| 'Gravettian' | | Kostienki XII, I.2 (Kostienki XVII, expected date) Molodova II (I.7) | Upper Perigordian | Upper Perigordian | Upper Perigordian |
| Perigordian (C) | | | | | |
| Evolved Aurignacian | 'Gravettian' | Molodova V | Aurignac. II | | Evolved Aurignacian |
| Szeletian (C) | Aurignacian Aurignacian I | | Aurignac. I | Aurignac. I | Aurignacian I |
| Aurignacian (C,A) Szeletian (C) | Szeletian | 'Gravettian' (?) | Lower Perigordian (?) | Lower Perigordian | |
| (Blattspitzen cultures) | | | | | |
| Mousterian | Mousterian | | Mousterian | | Mousterian |

probably outside influences – marked, if this is not a case of convergence – by the existence of Jermanovice points in the upper level of Kostienki I or the 'Western' look of the lower layer, and even the upper layer, of Kostienki IV.

In China Shui-tong-Kou provides an intermediate link between an extreme oriental Mousterian and Siberian Upper Palaeolithic.

In Africa, the Cyrenatean Upper Palaeolithic with its wealth of backed blades is certainly not derived from Lower Perigordian, with which it seems in the bottom layer to be more or less contemporary; but it may perhaps be derived from the backed blade industries at the bottom of Ksar'Akil.

In the Maghreb, the Aterian is likewise a kind of Upper Palaeolithic derived from Mousterian. South of the Sahara, Stillbay and Lupemban are in the same way industries that play the part of the Upper Palaeolithic, and are probably the work of modern men, though not related to European or Asiatic industries.

Even if progress in research makes it possible one day to reveal certain common origins for the central European (Szeletian) industry and certain of those in eastern Europe (Kostienki I – basal layer), it seems increasingly certain that the transition from Middle to Upper Palaeolithic – more or less concomitant with the transition from Neanderthal to modern man – took place at various places and at various times within a period that would appear to fall between 40 and 35,000 years before our era. And this is a fact anthropologists will have to reckon with in their study of man's 'physical evolution'.

We are probably dealing then with different origins; we are certainly dealing with different destinies; and it is not easy to understand the course followed by the various evolutions. In France, the Aurignacian and the Perigordian seem to disappear, having reached very evolved forms towards the end of Würm III, just before the development of the Solutrean, the origins of which are unknown. (Smith interprets this as a case of the retarded development of a prolonged Mousterian. But in the Rhône valley, according to Combier, the Lower Solutrean contains Perigordian elements.) Final Perigordian, Final Aurignacian and Lower Solutrean are all to be placed within a span of about 1,000 years, if we are to believe the dates obtained by $C^{14}$ at Laugerie-Haute. Early Magdalenian, replacing Solutrean – which in its turn suddenly vanished from the scene – seems to have no links with Perigordian, nor perhaps with the Final Aurignacian. After this Early Magdalenian (O + I), Magdalenian II seems to appear suddenly out of the blue. Backed bladelets, which were practically absent from Early Magdalenian, are here well developed and accompanied by microliths; and these characteristics might perhaps provide some links with Final Perigordian. But where did the latter go into hiding during the Solutrean/Early Magdalenian interregnum? After Magdalenian III, the Magdalenian goes on developing quite logically until its at least partial transformation into Azilian.

Outside France the sequence is often fragmentary and there are numerous gaps. In central Europe, we find industries analogous to the French (Vogelherd Aurignacian, Dolni Vestonice Perigordian) in spite of some original features. If the direction in which Aurignacian extended was perhaps from east to west, Perigordian certainly moved in the opposite direction and its influence perhaps made itself felt as far afield as Kostienki IV. But there are also industries that are clearly distinct: Jermanovician and Szeletian, which may go back to a common stock, take the place of the Lower Western Perigordian. Again, Willendorf 'Upper Perigordian' also clearly has affinities with the upper layer of Kostienki I; but lacking a more delicate scale of chronology, we do not know which comes before which. In the USSR the level containing triangular points at the bottom of Kostienki I seems to extend northwards in the site of

Sounghir, which is certainly more recent. Incidentally, if such an industry were to be found in Siberia, it would provide a good possible ancestor for the Palaeo-Indian industries of the Clovis Folsom type. The greatest surprise comes from the upper layer of the Telmanskaya site, where, after who can say how many thousands of years, the typical Jermanovice points crop up again, along with many other clearly Mousteroid forms as well as Upper Palaeolithic types. At Moldova v there is the development of a whole series of post-Mousterian industries, obviously descended from one another in certain layers but less clearly so in others. At Siuren II there is a recurrence in the Final Palaeolithic of points very like those in the Polish Final Palaeolithic, though at present it is not possible to understand the relationship between them. Although certain of these Russian industries contain Aurignacoid *features*, there is no *industry* that can be called Aurignacian, or even Aurignacoid. Nor is there any Solutrean, in spite of the bifacial leaf-shaped artifacts or the shouldered points of various types, which no doubt often represent convergenes. It is quite a different world from the western one, although the latter has sometimes made its influence felt (in Kostienki IV for instance) and although the men of Kostienki I (layer 1) certainly had relations with Austria and Czechoslovakia.

In Siberia it is again a different picture, looking to Asia rather than Europe for its origins. The stone industry remains more loaded with Mousterian memories. It may possibly be derived from an industry of the Shui-tong-Kou type. These Siberian industries seem to be rather late.

The Upper Palaeolithic in monsoon Asia is practically an unknown quantity. It seems probable that there, too, evolution started out from industries in the Mousterian stage. It should however be noted that there are industries with blades in Japan.

The Middle East on the other hand belongs to a large extent to the European tradition in which Mousterian memories quickly fade out. After Emirehan – which needs better definition – come a variety of industries, particularly at Ksar'Akil which do not always seem to run along the Palestinian Aurignacian line. But this Aurignacian culture is sometimes so like its Western counterpart that it is very difficult to call it by any other name. It certainly does possess peculiar features, but so does the German! so indeed does that of Corrèze in comparison with the classical forms of the Dordogne. It would appear to last on a long time and then pass over into the Mesolithic through a series of imperfectly-known industries having perhaps an outside origin. What is needed in the Middle East is new excavations carried out with special care to see that the stratigraphy is both delicate and accurate. At Ksar'Akil, overlying the Aurignacian, there is at least one level where the distribution of the type of tool follows the Early Magdalenian pattern although the *style* of these tools is different. This poses the problem of convergences at the level of industries and not merely types.

North Africa also has its blade industries of European type which are older in Egypt and more particularly in Cyrenaica than they are in the Maghreb. In the Maghreb, Upper Palaeolithic begins with an industry derived directly from the Mousterian, namely Aterian, which seems to evolve and last on very late south of the Sahara. It is only at a later stage that the country was occupied by blade and bladelet industries – Ibero-Maurusian, then Capsian, which was partly post-glacial and Epipalaeolithic. South of the Sahara, Lupem ban and Stillbay play a part similar to that of the Aterian, and then pass over into industries of the epipalaeolithic style.

At some indefinite moment – probably further back in time than has often been thought – peoples who were the bearers of industries, probably of the Siberian type, crossed the Bering Straits and so discovered America for the first time, long before Christopher

Columbus or the Vikings. The anonymous nature of this discovery, which means that we shall never know who was the first to set foot on what was to become the land of America, does not prevent this nameless person from being its true discoverer. In this unoccupied world, territorial expansion must have been rapid. It is more than probable that these migrations from Asia to America continued over a fairly long period, and involved various races and sub-races. The Palaeo-Indian cultures can be considered as Palaeolithic, even if they are partly post-glacial in the sense that they prolong the Palaeolithic way of life into a world which was itself an extended Palaeolithic world from the point of view of its fauna. The fact that these cultures sometimes resemble the Solutrean once again raises the problem of convergences.

The question of convergences in the Palaeolithic is extremely important and interesting. We saw that the Padjitanian bifacial implements are perhaps nothing but an example of convergent development, with no real relationship with Acheulean. This phenomenon of convergence stands out with particular clarity in the case of the leaf-shaped and shouldered points.

To begin with, one must eliminate a certain number of cases where the similarity only exists because of defective typology. A bifacial industry working with thin slabs as its raw material will easily manage to produce flat or leaf-shaped variants of bifacial tools that are elsewhere thicker in form. True leaf-shaped forms do appear sporadically in Acheulean and Mousterian cultures. They constitute an important part of the *Blattspitzen* Mousterian in Germany and of the Szeletian. In the latter case, there is a probable link of relationship. They are also to be found in the Jermanovician. In this industry, there are likewise unifacial forms resembling certain plane-face points in the Solutrean, 18,000 years later. The existence of these same types in the upper Jermanovice levels reduces this gap a little, but not enough to suggest derivation.

There is rather less doubtful, but still not absolutely certain, derivation between Jermanovice and the upper level of Telmanskaya; but here too the gap in time seems a large one, and there is a considerable distance in kilometres between these two places – about 1,300 as the crow flies. As the Jermanovice assemblage – apart from the points – is very poor, this problem can probably only be solved by some intermediate sites being discovered. There are Jermanovice points in the upper layer of Kostienki ɪ, as there are at Telmanskaya; and here the time interval is much smaller, and we are dealing with the same region. But at Kostienki ɪ these points may only be a preliminary stage in the fabrication of shouldered points. It is possible that these shouldered points did actually develop out of the Jermanovice ones; but here too it may simply be a question of convergence.

Leaf-shaped points are to be met with in French Solutrean, North African Aterian, Stillbay, and Lupemban, in the Palaeo-Indian industries, in Australia, etc. It can only be a question of convergences. But there is surely no law preventing convergences from showing up in places that are close to one another just as much as in distant ones. It will always be very rash to talk of affinities and influences as between one industry and another on the basis of a single type. It would not be difficult to multiply examples. There are concave base points in Spanish Solutrean, and in the industries of America. Again, there are abundant leaf-shaped points in the Chalcolithic, which is not derived from the Solutrean. In southern Spain, there are tanged and barbed points of Neolithic style in the Solutrean, etc., etc.

The shouldered point is another type apt to be independently invented at various times and in various places. These points are met with in the Upper Perigordian; then they disappear during the whole of Lower and Middle Solutrean, only to reappear in another form in Upper Solutrean. Then they vanish once again, but reappear in yet another style during Upper Magdalenian or Hamburgian. It is the same with the tanged points, invented by the Font-Robert type Perigordians, forgotten, then rediscovered in Upper Magdalenian or nordic Final Palaeolithic. One might instance the 'Perigordian' burins at El Inga in Ecuador, or the Danish Neolithic axes with their very special features, which turn up again with all their complicated fabrication technique in the Neolithic of Java!

We must therefore be very cautious in talking of diffusion or influence. The Siuren II points in the Crimea are like the Polish Masovian points, and this resemblance has sometimes led to talk of mutual influence; but nothing could be more uncertain. Interestingly enough, these points, while smaller, are rather similar in type to the Jermanovice points. It is therefore as well to base our arguments on bulk comparisons and not on isolated types. For instance, according to the fine material published by Klima, the Dolni-Vestonice Perigordian is like that at Corbiac (Dordogne) because *all* the types in one are also, with very few exceptions, to be found in the other, *in very similar proportions* and with the *same general style*.

The machinery of convergence is fairly easy to explain in the case of the plane-faced points (see figure 74). What is needed is to obtain a projectile point or a pointed knife – it does not matter which – rectilinear in one plane if possible, and with a handle. The pointed shape conditions the form of the further end. The handle can be fitted on either by means of a tang (this is not the case here), or by means of a simple narrowing down. If the wood available for the handle is elastic enough, the existence of the percussion bulb – already reduced by the retouching necessary for narrowing it down – will not matter; but if the wood has less 'give' in it, or if it is a bone handle, it will be more convenient to remove the bulb and so thin down the part next to it. Finally, the flake is

*Figure 74* Mechanism and examples of convergences. 1, desired
shape; 2, obtaining the shape from a flake; 3, on the flat face
the bulb still exists, and the blade is curved; 4, removal
of the bulb and straightening of the point; 5, Solutrean; 6, Siuren II;
7, Masovian point; 8, point found in level XVI of Ksar' Akil.

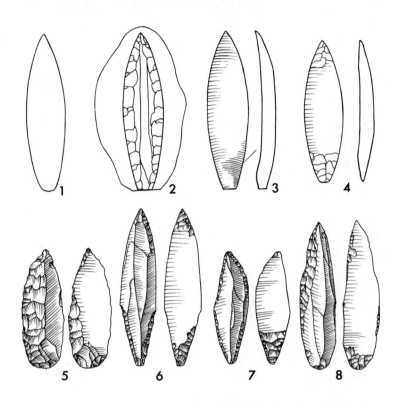

straightened if need be by retouching the further end on its flat
surface. This is a series of technical procedures which can certainly
be rediscovered at various points, existing in scattered form or
otherwise carried out on other types of tool (for example the
thinned-down base of certain Mousterian points, or on the
Emireh points, or the pointing of the far end or the removal of the
bulb by retouching on the flat face of numerous Gravette points,
etc.). This same series of technical operations when applied to

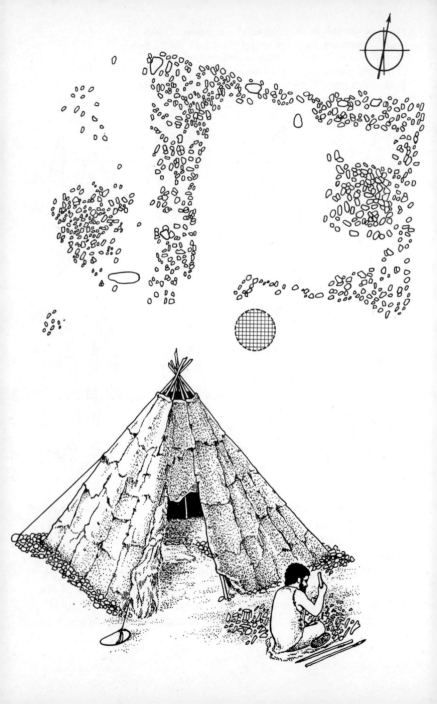

*Figure 75* (*Above*) Position of the pebbles at Plateau Parrain. The shaded circle shows the place of a heap of flakes. Left, one of the workshops, marked by other pebbles. Inside, a pavement CA. one square metre. (*Below*) Reconstruction of this tent. *Figure 76 A–B* (*Above*) Site of a tent at Plateau Parrain (Dordogne), marked by the pebbles which surrounded it. (*Below*) Pavement of another Magdalenian tent at Cerisier (Dordogne). (Excavations by J. Gaussen.)

blades will produce Siuren or Masovian points without there being any need to have recourse to the explanation of contacts or traditions. The case of the tanged point is equally simple. An interesting example is concerned with the backed bladelets and the so-called Dufour bladelets. The latter occur especially in the Aurignacian. They are often warped bladelets, semi-steeply retouched, and exist in three types:

1 with alternate retouching (figure 56, 6). This is the type for which the label 'Dufour' ought really to be kept;
2 retouched on one edge, inverse;
3 retouched on one edge, dorsal.

This last type passes over imperceptibly, when the retouching becomes more abrupt, into a backed bladelet, without any need to invoke possible contacts with the Perigordian. This is quite certainly the case at Krems. Among true backed bladelets the back itself is variable in thickness and steepness. Inverse unilateral retouching also exists in the Perigordian, although it is rare. But the backed blades fairly often have the edge opposite to the back trimmed by means of delicate direct or inverse retouching. In the latter case, if the back is of the less steep type, one has a Dufour bladelet without any need for contact with the Aurignacian.

It will therefore not be easy to unravel all the possible influences. In the Perigordian, there are some carinated end-scrapers in a style generally differing from the Aurignacian ones. A good number are probably the result of convergences, such as end-scrapers made on thick flakes by the technique that produces bladelets from a core. Others perhaps reveal certain contacts or intermarriages, so to speak. But sometimes the contact may be posthumous, for Palaeolithic men picked up objects of an earlier period and these may well have given them ideas.

The rarity of discoverable contacts between different cultures opens up the question of habitats and migrations, and the density of population. We must not model our thinking about the Palaeo-lithic world on the world as we know it today, overpopulated as it is except in the zones that are unfavourable to life. The Palaeolithic world might be described as a human desert swarming with game. The zones in which the last tribes of hunters and gatherers have taken refuge today only serve to put wrong ideas in our heads, for Europe – except in certain regions – has never been like the Kalahari or the Australian deserts where the last of the bushmen or the aborigines wander and (culturally speaking, at least) are in course of extinction. The environment then was certainly capable of supporting a much denser population; but there were various unfavourable factors that hindered demographic development over a long period. First, there was the uncertainty as to food though this was no doubt less important than has been imagined; then there was probably a very high rate of infant mortality, and epidemics which must sometimes have destroyed whole tribes. During the most favourable period, the Upper Magdalenian, the population of France can hardly have exceeded a few tens of thousands – 50,000 at most; but perhaps fairly well concentrated. During the Mousterian, the population was no doubt much smaller. This demographic expansion was doubtless irregular, with marked ups and downs, which may not have all taken place at the same time in different regions. A man may well have lived all his life without more than a rare meeting with anyone from another tribe, let alone of another culture; and it is very possible that these contacts, when they did take place, were not always peaceful or fruitful. However, the unity of Palaeolithic art in the south-west of France suggests that at any rate in the Magdalenian period contacts between Perigord and the Pyrenees must have been fairly sustained. There is another reason which must have made contacts other than voluntary ones a rare event. Far from leading a cease-lessly nomadic life, as was commonly supposed after the example of

*Figure 77* Two Magdalenian hearths
at Pincevent, near Paris. Near
the hearths, a big stone
was used as a seat. On the
ground, numerous flints and bones.

the Bushmen and the Australian aborigines, it would seem that Palaeolithic man – sometimes even as early as the Acheulean – was fairly settled. The thickness of the layers containing a single industry from top to bottom was already a pointer in this direction; and J. Bouchud's work on the reindeer's dentition has shown that early man occupied the shelters throughout the year, or at least part of the tribe did so. He can only have changed his encampment when forced to do so, when for some reason or other the hunting became too poor, which could only have happened in Palaeolithic conditions after a given zone had been exploited over a long period. And the change of camping-site no doubt took place within the confines of a particular territory. But as well as the

*Figure 78* A lower Solutrean hearth at Laugerie-Haute. Pebbles inside were probably used to keep the place radiating heat after the fire was burnt out.

permanent camps there were also no doubt temporary open-air encampments, as we shall see later on. Towards the end of the Magdalenian period, in Magdalenian VI, a kind of population explosion seems to have taken place, the causes of which are interesting to examine. There are a great many impressive Magdalenian VI sites, and when this Magdalenian VI occupies the same shelter as older levels, the surface occupied is much larger and spreads a good distance round about the shelter. This is the moment when light weapons begin to appear (shouldered points, Laugerie-Basse points, and Teyjat points); and one would imagine that this, like the growth of the population, was bound up with the invention of the bow, which made hunting more profitable. At the same time, spear-throwers seem to dwindle or disappear. Another factor may have been the development of fishing for salmonidae, numerous backbones of which have been found, though these fish were consumed much earlier on; or perhaps it was the invention of a means of preserving meat and fish, such as smoking or drying. This Final Magdalenian gives the impression of a civilisation undergoing expansion, an expansion that was to be cut short by the changed climate of the Postglacial period. We should note towards the end of the Palaeolithic period a general tendency for the implements to become microlithic and a development of geometric flints, probably in connection with the manufacture of complex weapon points.

There was great variety of habitat in the Upper Palaeolithic, as was already the case in the Mousterian. Man probably began to make rock-shelters more habitable. Tree-trunks were felled by lighting a bonfire at the foot and then propping them up against the rock-face, where they were trellised by branches and skins, thus constituting fairly comfortable huts that were relatively easy to keep warm. The existence of heating is sometimes revealed by variations in the character of the sediment. On other occasions and in the case of larger caves, huts or tents were no doubt built inside them. Traces of these arrangements have been found at various sites: Arcy-sur-Cure in Lower Perigordian, la Salpétrière in Lower Solutrean, le Pech-de-la-Boisière and le Fourneau du Diable in Upper Solutrean. But there are also open-air dwelling-sites (probably in tents) in the Mussidan region of the Dordogne (figures 75, 76). In this place Gaussen has found traces of various Magdalenian habitats. On the Parrain plateau, there was a rectangular line of pebbles, probably placed on the skirts of the tent-skins; and inside there was a small partially paved area. Round the tent there were various 'workshops', to judge by the position of flakes, blades, tools, etc. In other places there are rectangles of varying dimensions paved with pebbles, sometimes with appendices at either end. The Solvieux site is different in type. It consists of a huge pebble paving, with abundant remains of Magdalenian industry, situated at a short distance from a river. Was this a fisherman's camp, with a place for drying fish? Temporary dwelling-places like this have long been described by Rust in the north of Germany; and it would seem that the tent layout varied according to the type of industry represented. Leroi-Gourhan's excavations at Pincevent (Seine-et-Marne) have led to the discovery of a Magdalenian site with hearths still in position (figure 77).

These open-air dwelling-places, which were common in Magdalenian times, already existed in the Perigordian, as witnessed by the large deposits, sometimes with many layers, to be found round about Bergerac. At Rabier, for instance, a deposit of this type was excavated in 1965 by J. and G. Guichard, who produced clear evidence of concentrations of various types of tools corresponding to a division of work. Unfortunately in these acid sands the fauna has not been preserved. At Rabier there is a very extensive layer, but it is thin, and probably indicates that the period of occupation was short. In other places such as Corbiac it seems that the Upper

Perigordians had a summer camp there for many years on end.

Sites of the same type also exist at Saut-du-Perron (Loire) and probably at many other places.

In central and eastern Europe, where rock-shelters are relatively rare, the men of Upper Palaeolithic times have left important traces of permanent habitats in the loess, particularly in the USSR. These habitations are of various types. There are traces of round or oval huts from four to six metres in diameter, with a central hearth. Sometimes these are slightly hollowed out in the soil of the period, and the walls are supported by the bones of large animals or slabs of stone. These huts were probably covered with skins, as at Gargarino, for instance. Others are long-shaped, sometimes being sunk in the soil; for example the one at Pushkhari, which measures 12 by 4 metres. Some of them are very large – at Kostienki I for example; where there are traces of two habitats, each 35 by 15 metres, and not sunk in the ground. There were nine hearths situated on the longer axis, and numerous silos varying in shape and height, some of them with narrow mouths. It does not seem likely that all this could have been covered in under one single roof.

The Upper Palaeolithic period in Europe also saw a great development of art; but as a book in this series already deals particularly with this subject* we shall not enlarge on it here, nor shall we examine its significance either as pure art, or as magic, or as symbolism. But its existence, and the numerous funerary rites observed in the burials, add to the feeling of great complexity aroused by these Palaeolithic societies. It is possible that Upper Palaeolithic men already possessed a lunar calendar, either in connection with a whole mythology or perhaps for practical ends, as suggested by the as yet largely unpublished researches of

---

*Palaeolithic Cave Art*, by Peter J. Ucko and Andrée Rosenfeld.

M.A.Marshack. Much of these men's daily life will for ever remain unknown to us: their social and family organisation, their songs and dances – although a faint light is cast on the latter now and again either by parietal drawings or by footprints in certain caves. One cannot help wondering how far these hunting societies would have advanced along the road to civilisation if post-glacial conditions had not so abruptly put an end to their progress.

# Glossary

| | |
|---|---|
| Aeolian deposits | Wind-blown deposits characteristic of relatively dry periods e.g. interpluvials or glacials with low precipitation. |
| Anvil (*or* Block on Block technique) | Method of removing flakes by swinging the core against an anvil. Produces large thick flakes. Used extensively in the Clactonian culture. |
| Artifact | Any man-made object. |
| Backed blade | Blade tool blunted on side opposite to edge by removal of small steep flakes. |
| Bâton de Commandement | Implement made from antler with a cylindrical hole at one end. Often decorated, dating from the Aurignacian to the Upper Magdalenian. Interpretations vary from the symbolic to it being a spear-thrower or arrow-straightener. |
| Bifacial Tool | Artifact that has been flaked on both sides. |
| Bipolar Technique | Core is placed on an anvil and flake is detached by striking with a third implement. Characterised by double bulb of percussion, one at each end of the flake or, more often on quartz tacts, by crushing at each end. |
| Blade tools | Tool made from a single thin narrow flake detached from a core. Controlled flaking technique characteristic of the Upper Palaeolithic but also known from earlier cultures. |
| Breccia | Conglomerate of rock and detritus consolidated by carbonate of lime into a hard bed. |
| Bulb of Percussion | Bulb left on the flake surface at the impact point on the striking platform. |
| Burin | Tool with a transverse (chisel) edge made by the removal of one or more flakes. Used for working bone, antler and ivory, and perhaps for engraving. Common in the Upper Palaeolithic. |
| Chopper | Large unifacial tool with the cutting edge flaked from only one side. |
| Chopping tool | Bifacial core tool with sinuous, transverse edge |

caused by alternate flaking. Characteristic
Palaeolithic type especially in all Mid-Pleistocene
Asian industries.

Cleaver — Roughly U-shaped tool with a transverse cutting
edge. Bifacial cleavers resemble truncated handaxes
with a straight or oblique edge at the tip. On flake
cleavers the cutting edge is generally formed by the
intersection of the primary flake surface and a
transverse flake seat on the upper surface, i.e. a
'tranchet' blow.

Colluvium — Hill-Wash material.

Cordiformes — Heart-shaped handaxes characteristic of the
Mousterian industries of Acheulean tradition.

Cranial capacity — Volume of the brain expressed in cubic centimetres.

Cryoturbation — Convection currents and pressure of ice crystals in
the refrozen subsoil after a seasonal thaw, rotates
stones and soil, and results in structured soils.
Indicative of Arctic climatic conditions.

Cylindrical Hammer Technique — Removal of shallow flakes in the manufacture of
handaxes and other tools, by using an implement of
a softer material (wood or bone) than the tool itself.
Characteristic of the Acheulean and later cultures,
often used as a means of distinguishing the
Acheulean from the Abbevillian.

Discoidal cores — Prepared cores of the Mousterian from which
flakes have been detached. Discarded when it
becomes too small.

Dufour Bladelets — Small bladelets with semi-abrupt alternating
retouching along one or both sides.

End-scraper — Narrow blade tool with a convex working edge at
one or both ends.

Endocranial cast — Cast made of the interior of the skull, principally
to show the marks left by the cortex area of the
brain.

Epi-palaeolithic — Cultures of Palaeolithic tradition surviving into the

| | |
|---|---|
| | early Postglacial. |
| Fenho complex | Chinese Palaeolithic cultures of the early Upper Pleistocene. |
| First intermediate | Period between the Earlier and Middle Stone Ages in Africa. Dated to about 40,000 years ago. |
| Foliated points (*Blattspitzen*) | Elliptical shaped points, thin in section and pointed at both ends. Reminiscent of Solutrean 'laurel leaves' but forms part of the Mousterian assemblages of central Europe. |
| Font-Robert points | Tanged points with leaf-shaped blades of plano-convex section. Only worked extensively on one face. Dated to Perigordian v in France. |
| Gamblian | Last major pluvial period of the Pleistocene in Africa. |
| Geometric microliths | Small blade tools of geometric form usually having a point or transverse edge. Almost certainly hafted, possibly forming composite tools and weapons. Characteristic of the Mesolithic but do begin to appear by the end of the Upper Palaeolithic |
| Great interglacial | Mindel/Riss phase dated to the Middle Pleistocene. Also called Elster-Saale or Hoxnian. |
| Günz Glaciation | First glaciation of the Pleistocene in the Alps. |
| Handaxes | Pear-shaped or ovoid stone tool, bifacially worked. Characteristic of the Abbevillian and Acheulean industries in Europe and the Chelles-Acheul in Africa. |
| Hollow-scraper | Blade or flake tool with a notch in the side or end showing signs of being worked. |
| Interpluvial | Period when the rainfall was less than it is at present. |
| Inverse retouch | Retouching done by direct or indirect percussion technique, working from the top of the flake so that chips are removed from its smooth underside. |
| Isostasy | Mechanism by which the equilibrium of the continents as Sial blocks is maintained in the |

Sima levels of the earth's crust. Severely affected by the added pressure of the ice sheets during the Pleistocene.

Jermanovice Points
Laurel-leaf points, flaked completely on one side but bifacially only on the lower part of the blade and on the bulb of percussion. Characteristic of the Upper Palaeolithic Jermanovice culture in Poland.

Kageran
Formerly the first pluvial period dated to the Lower Pleistocene. Now more or less abandoned or incorporated with the Kamasian.

Kamasian
Second Pluvial period in Africa, dated to the Middle Pleistocene.

Kanjeran
Third pluvial period in Africa, dated to the later part of the Middle Pleistocene.

Knives
*see* backed blades.

Lanceolate
Lance- or lozenge-shaped. Tapering at both ends.

Laterite
Ferruginous rock formed *in situ* by weathering of basic rocks under wet tropical conditions. If eroded and re-deposited called detrital laterite.

Levallois Technique
Prepared core technique of producing flake tools, evolved during late Acheulean times and characteristic of many Mousterian cultures.

Limace
Blade tool retouched along both sides to form a 'slug-shaped' object.

Loess
Deposits of rock dust carried by the wind in arid conditions, for instance during glacial period, from exposed glacial moraines and outwash deposits.

Micro-burin
Residual product in the fabrication of microliths by the 'notched blade' technique. Has no functional purpose.

Micro-burin technique (or notched-blade technique)
Production of microliths by notching the blade on one side and snapping it. This gives the waste product called micro-burin and a short segment of blade from which the microlith can be made.

Mindel
Second major glacial period of the Pleistocene in

| | the Alps. |
|---|---|
| Mladec/Lautch points | Large lozenge-shaped bone points from cave of same name in Czechoslovakia, belonging to the Aurignacian. |
| Noailles gravers | Small gravers made from thin, flat blades, truncated and retouched to give multiple gravers. Dated to Perigordian vc in France. |
| Obsidian | Volcanic glass that has many of the flaking qualities of flint. |
| Ovates | Ovate handaxes—elliptical in shape, relatively thin in section, sometimes with a twisted edge due to alternate flaking. |
| Pedology | Study and analysis of soils. |
| Percussion technique | Direct striking of core with a hammer-stone, giving thick bulbous flakes, or with a cylindrical (bone or wooden) hammer, giving flatter flakes. Indirect percussion or Punch technique necessitated the use of a bone or wooden punch between the hammer and the core, controlling the precision of flaking. |
| Periglacial | Arctic conditions of the regions surrounding an ice sheet. |
| Picks | Long narrow core tools, sometimes slightly curved in profile, truncated at one end and pointed at the other. Typical of the Sangoan in Africa. |
| Pleistocene | Period within the Quaternary defined by the palaeontological evidence. Often, incorrectly, correlated only to the Great Ice Ages which it includes and which act as a means of subdivision. |
| Pliocene | Last period of the Tertiary era, dating from about 14–2 million years ago. |
| Pluvial | Period when the rainfall was greater than it is at present. |
| Pollen analysis | Study of the plant life of a certain period by the remains of pollen grains found in the soils of the same period. The proportions of pollen give an |

| | |
|---|---|
| | ınuıcatıon of the type and proportion of flora existing. |
| Potassium argon dating | Radioactive absolute dating method applicable to volcanic rocks. |
| Quaternary | The Post-Pliocene periods, composed of the Pleistocene and the Holocene or Recent. Formerly dated to 1 million years, now includes the Villafranchian period and dated at Olduvai to more than 2 million years ago. |
| Radiocarbon dating (Carbon 14) | Method of Absolute dating, based on the rate of radioactive decay of the isotope Carbon 14 contained in organic material. Accurate only up to about 70,000 years. |
| Relative dating | The age of a specimen relative to its position in a stratigraphical or archaeological sequence. Dating by geological strata, related faunas or morphological sequence is included in this system. |
| Riss | Third major glacial period of the Pleistocene in the Alps. |
| Scalar retouch | Retouch done in such a way as to resemble the scales of a fish. |
| Side-scraper | Scraper made by retouching one or more edges of a fluke. |
| Solifluction | In periglacial conditions the subsoil is permanently frozen. During the seasonal thaw, the top layer thaws and, since the water cannot drain, forms a sludge which flows down to the lowest point available. |
| Spheroids | Chipped spherical missiles either thrown or slung, or possibly used as a form of bolas. |
| Strangulated blade scraper | Long blade tool with a retouched notch on one or both sides. Possibly used as a wood-working tool like a modern spokeshave. Characteristic of the Aurignacian. |
| Striking platform | Point on a core, at right angles to the intended line |

| | of the flake, which is struck to detach this flake. |
|---|---|
| Supra-orbital torus | A protruding bony brow-ridge, frequently found in early forms of man and most marked in male gorillas. |
| Taiga | A slightly more temperate vegetation than tundra. Composed of stunted forest, mainly coniferous, on frozen subsoil. Probably much more extensive than tundra in Periglacial Europe. |
| Tectonic movements | Movements in the earth's crust which result in such structural features as the folding or faulting of rocks and the uplift or sinking of part of the earth's surface. |
| Tertiary | The oldest period of the Cenozoic era, following the Cretaceous period and preceding the Quaternary. |
| Thumb-nail scrapers | Round scrapers on small flakes or ends of blades; known to have been hafted in certain cases by traces of resin on specimens. |
| Tjaele | Also called permafrost. Conditions by which subsoil is permanently frozen under perigacial conditions. |
| Tranchets | Tools having a straight cutting edge caused by the removal of a flake parallel with the cutting edge. |
| Travertines | Calcareous beds laid down by water action, especially by springs. |
| Tufas | Calcareous deposits left by springs. Used as indicators of consistent rainfall in now arid areas. |
| Tuffs | Volcanic deposits of fragmentary rock and volcanic dust when solidified. Sometimes used as a source of raw material. |
| Tundra | Periglacial type of environment with subsoil permanently frozen – vegetation restricted to mosses, small plants, shrubs etc. |
| Unifacial tool | Artifact that has been flaked only on one side. |
| Varve analysis | The annual melting of the ice during the Pleistocene |

gave rise to a regular cycle of glacial lake deposits which can be counted. De Geer and his colleagues were able to establish a reasonably complete chronology for Scandinavia during this period.

Victoria West Technique (Proto- or Para-Levallois)

A variant of the Levallois (prepared core) technique in which the blow to remove the flake is given on the side of the core. Produces short wide flakes, often transformed in flake cleavers in the African Acheulean.

Villafranchian

Formerly classed as Upper Pliocene, now included in the Lower Pleistocene.

Würm

Fourth major glacial period of the Pleistocene in the Alps.

# Bibliography

**General works, quaternary geology and human palaeontology.**

Blanc (A.C.). *Origine e sviluppo dei popoli cacciatori e raccoglitori*. Rome, 1956.

Bonifay (E.). *Les terrains quaternaires dans le Sud-Est de la France*. Bordeaux, 1962.

Bordes (F.). *Les limons quaternaires du Bassin de la Seine*. Paris, 1953.

Bordes (F.). *Typologie du Paléolithique ancien et moyen*. 2 vols. Bordeaux, 1961.

Breuil (H.). 'De l'importance de la solifluxion dans l'étude des terrains quaternaires du Nord de la France et des pays voisins'. *Revue de Géographie physique et de Géologie dynamique*. Paris, 1934, vol. VII, fasc. 4.

Breuil (H.). *Beyond the bounds of History*. London, 1949.

Brothwell (D.) and Higgs (E.) eds. *Science in Archeology*. London, 1963. American edition, New York, 1963.

Butzer (K.W.). *Environment in Archaeology*. Chicago, 1964.

Cailleux (A.) and Taylor (G.). *Crypédologie*. Paris, 1954.

Caldwell (J.H.) ed. *New Roads to Yesterday*. New York, 1966.

Clark (J.D.) and Howell (F.C.) eds. 'Recent studies in Paleoanthropology'. *American Anthropologist*, April, 1966.

Duchaufour (P.H.). *Précis de Pédologie*. Paris, 1960.

Fischer (F.) and Kimmig (W.) eds. *Festschrift Gustav Riek. Fundberichte aus Schwaben*, Neue Folge, 17, Stuttgart, 1965.

Flint (R.F.). *Glacial and Pleistocene geology*. New York, London, Sydney; 4th edition, 1964.

Freund (G.) ed. *Festschrift für Lothar Zotz*. Bonn, 1960.

Heinzelin (J. de). *Manuel de typologie des industries lithiques*. Institut Royal des Sciences Naturelles de Belgique. Bruxelles, 1962.

Heizer (R.F.) and Cook (S.F.) eds. *The application of quantitive methods in archaeology*. Chicago, 1960.

'Homage to S. Brodar.' *Archeološki Vestnik*, *XIII–XIV*, Ljubljana, 1962–3.

Howell (F.C.). *Early Man*. Life Nature Library, Amsterdam, 1965.

Koenigswald (G.H.R. von) ed. *Neandertal Centenary*. Wenner-Gren Foundation, Utrecht, 1958.

Kroeber (A.L.). *Anthropology*, New York, 1948; English edn. London, 1948.

Lavocat (R.) ed. *Faunes et flores préhistoriques*. Paris, 1966.

Oakley (K.). *Frameworks for dating fossil man*. London, 1964.

Piveteau (J.). *Paléontologie humaine. Traité de Paléontologie*, vol. VII, Paris, 1957.

'Pleistocene Research'. *Bulletin of the Geological Society of America*, vol. 60, no. 9, Sept. 1949.

Ripoll Perello (E.) ed. *Miscelánea en Homenaje al abate Henri Breuil*. Diputacion provincial de Barcelona, 2 vols., 1965.

Semenov (S. A.). *Prehistoric technology*. London, 1964.

Sonneville-Bordes (D. de). *L'Age de la Pierre*. Paris, 1961.

Tax (S.) ed. *The evolution of man*. (Evolution after Darwin, the University of Chicago centennial.) Chicago, 1960.

Tax (S.) ed. *Horizons in Anthropology*, Chicago, 1964; English edn. London, 1965.

Washburn (S.) ed. *Social life of early man*. Chicago, 1961; English edn. London, 1962.

Washburn (S.) ed. *Classification and human evolution*. Chicago, 1963; English edn. London, 1964.

## Europe.

Barta (J.). *Slovenško v staršej a strednej dobe kammenej* (Die Slowakei in der Älteren und Mittleren Steinzeit). (German summary). Bratislava, 1965.

Bartucz (L.), Dancza (J.), Hollendonner (F.), Kadic (O.), Mottl (M.), Pataki (V.), Palosi (E.), Szabo (J.), Vendl (L.). 'Die Mussolini-Höhle (Subalyuk) bei Cserepfalu'. *Geologica hungarica, ser. Paleontologica*. Budapest, 1940.

Behm-Blancke (G.). 'Alsteinzeitliche Rastplätze im Travertingebiet von Taubach, Weimar, Ehringsdorf'. *Alt-Thüringen*, Band 4, 1960.

Blanc (A.C.). Torre in Pietra, Saccopastore e Monte Circeo. 'La cromologica dei giacimenti e la paleogeografia quaternalia del Lazio'. *Boll. Soc. Geogr. It.* 4–5. 1958.

Blanc (A.C.) and Segre (A.G.). *Excursion au Mont Circé* – Guide-book of the Fourth International Congress of INQUA, Rome, 1953.

Blanc (A.C.) and Segre (A.G.). *Excursion dans les Abrusses, les Pouilles et sur la côte de Salermo* – Guide-book of the Fourth International Congress of INQUA, Rome, 1953.

Bonch-Osmolovsky (G.A.). 'Grot Kiik-Koba'. *Paleolit Kryma I*, Moscow-Leningrad, 1940.

Bordes (F.) and Fitte (P.). 'L'atelier Commont'. *L'Anthropologie*, vol. 57, 1953.

Boriskovsky (P.I.). 'Ocherki po paleolitu basseina Dona'. *Materialy i issledovaniya po archeologhii SSSR*, No. 121, Moscow, 1963.

Boriskovsky (P.I.). 'Le Paléolithique de l'Ukraine'. (French translation).

*Annales du service d'information géologique*, N0. 27, Paris, 1958.

Bourdier (F.). *Le bassin du Rhône au Quaternaire*. Centre National de la Recherche scientifique, 2 vols. Paris, 1961.

Bourgon (M.). *Les industries moustériennes et pré-moustériennes du Périgord*. Paris, 1957.

Capitan (L.) and Peyrony (D.). *La Madeleine*. Publications de l'Institut international d'Anthropologie, No. 2, Paris, 1928.

Chernych (A.P.P.). 'Pozdny Paleolit srednego pridneistrovia'. *Trudy Komissii po izucheniu chetvertichogo perioda*. Moscow, 1959.

Clark (J.G.D.). *Excavations at Star Carr*. Cambridge, 1954.

Commont (V.). 'Les hommes contemporains du renne dans la vallée de la Somme'. *Société des Antiquaires de Picardie*, 1913.

Efimienko (P.P.). 'Kostienki I.' *Akademia Nauk SSSR, Institut Istorii materialnoi kultury*. Moscow, 1958.

Felgenhauer (F.). 'Willendorf in der Wachau'. *Mitteilungen der prähistorischen Kommission der Österreichischen Akademie der Wissenschaften*. Vienna, 1956–9.

Formosov (A.A.). 'Pechernaya Stoianka Starocelie'. *Materialy i issledovaniya po archeologii SSSR*, No. 71, Moscow, 1958.

Freund (G.). *Die Blattspitzen des Paläolithikums in Europa*. Bonn, 1952.

Grahmann (R.). 'The lower Palaeolithic site of Markkleeberg and other comparable localities near Leipzig'. *Transactions of the American Philosophical Society*, vol. 45, part. 6, 1955.

Klein (E.). *The Mousterian of European Russia*. Doctoral dissertation, mim. University of Chicago, 1966.

Klima (B.). 'Dolni Vestonice'. (With a German summary). *Monumenta archaeologica*, Prague, 1963.

Leonardi (P.) and Broglio (A.). *Le Paléolithique de la Venetie* – Annali Universitá di Ferrara, N.S., Section XV, 1962.

Obermaier (H.). *El Hombre fosil*. Museo nacional de Ciencas naturales, 2nd edn, Madrid, 1925. American edn. *Fossil Man in Spain*. The Hispanic Society of America, New Haven, 1924.

Okladnikov (ed.). *Paléolithique et Néolithique de l'U.R.S.S.* (French translation). Annales du Centre d'Etude et de documentation paléontologique, Paris, 1956.

Pericot Garcia (L.). *Historia de Espana*, vol. 1, Instituto Gallach de Libreria y ediciones, Barcelona, 1958.

Peyrony (D.). *Les gisements préhistoriques de Bourdeilles (Dordogne)*. Paris, 1932.

Peyrony (D. and E.). *Laugerie-Haute, près des Eyzies (Dordogne)*. Paris, 1938. *Piccola Guida della Preistoria Italiana*. Florence 2nd edn. 1965.

Radmilli (A.M.). *La Preistoria d'Italia alla luce delle ultime scoperte*.

Instituto geografico militare, Florence, 1963.

Riek (G.). *Die Eiszeitjägerstation am Vogelherd im Lonetal.* Tübingen, 1934.

Rogachev (A.N.). 'Kostienki IV.' *Materialy i issledovaniya po archeologhii SSSR*, No. 45, Moscow, 1955.

Rust (A.). *Die jungpaläolithischen Zeltanlagen von Ahrensburg.* Neumünster, 1954.

Rust (A.). *Artefakte aus der Zeit des Homo Heidelbergensis in Süd-und Norddeutschland.* Bonn, 1956.

Rust (A.). *Die Funde vom Pinneberg.* Neumünster, 1958.

Rust (A.). *Die Artefakte der Altonaer Stufe von Wittenbergen.* Nemünster, 1962.

Schwabedissen (H.). *Die Federmesser-Gruppen des nordwesteuropäischen Flachlandes.* Neumünster, 1954.

Shovkoplias (I.G.). *Mezinskiya Stoianka.* Akademiya Nauk Ukrainskoi SSSR, Kiev, 1965.

Smith (P.E.L.). *Le Solutréen en France.* Bordeaux, 1966.

Sonneville-Bordes (D.de). *Le Paléolithique supérieur en Périgord.* 2 vols, Bordeaux, 1960.

Vaufrey (R.). *Le Paléolithique italien.* Paris, 1928.

Vértes (L.). 'Neuere Ausgrabungen und paläolithische Funde in der Höhle von Istállóskó. *Acta archaelogica*, Budapest, 1964.

Vértes (L.). 'Tata'. *Archaeologia hungarica*, Budapest, 1964.

Zebera (K.). *Československo ve starši době Kammené* (Die Tschechoslowakei in der Alteren Steinzeit). (German summary). Ústřední ústav Geologiehý, Prague, 1958.

Zotz (L.). *Altsteinzeitkunde Mitteleuropas.* Stuttgart, 1951.

Zotz (L.). *Das Paläolithikum in den Weinberghöhlen bei Mauern.* Quartär-Bibliothek, vol. 2, Bonn, 1955.

**Africa.**

*Actes du IVème Congrès panafricain de Préhistoire et de l'Étude du Quaternaire.*
(Section III). Musée Royal de l'Afrique Centrale, Tervuren, Belgium, 1962.

Arkell (A.J.). *Wanyanga, and an archaeological reconnaissance of the south-west Libyan desert.* London, 1964.

Balout (L.). *Préhistoire de l'Afrique du Nord.* Paris, 1955.

Biberson (P.). 'Le cadre paléogéographique de la Préhistoire du Maroc atlantique'. *Service des Antiquités du Maroc*, fasc. 16. Rabat, 1961.

Chavaillon (J.). *Les formations quaternaires du Sahara Nord-Occidental.* Centre national de la Recherche scientifique, Paris, 1964.

Clark (J.D.). *The Prehistory of Southern Africa.* London, 1959.

Clark (J.D.). *Prehistoric cultures of north-east Angola and their significance in tropical Africa*. Lisbon, 1963.

Clark (J.D.). *The distribution of prehistoric cultures in Angola*. Lisbon, 1966.

Cole (S.). *The Prehistory of East Africa*. London, 1964.

Heinzelin (J. de). *Le Paléolithique aux abords d'Ishango*. Institut des Parcs nationaux du Congo, Brussells, 1961.

Howell (F.C.) and Bourlière (F.) eds. *African Ecology and human evolution*. Chicago, 1963; English edn. London, 1964.

Leakey (L.). *Olduvai Gorge*, Cambridge, 1951.

Leakey (L.). *Olduvai Gorge, 1951–61*. Cambridge, 1965.

McBurney (C.B.). *The Stone Age of Northern Africa*. London, 1960.

Vaufrey (R.). *Préhistoire de l'Afrique. I, Maghreb*. Paris, 1955.

### Asia, Oceania and America

Bordes (F.). 'Le Pré-Aurignacien de Yabroud (Syrie) et son incidence sur la Chronologie du Quaternaire en Moyen-Orient'. *Bulletin of the Research Council of Israel*, vol. 9G, 1960.

Bostanci (E.Y.). 'Research on the Mediterranean coast of Anatolia. A new Palaeolithic site at Beldibi near Antalya'. *Anatolia*, IV, Ankara, 1959.

Bostanci (E.Y.). 'Research in South-East Anatolia. The Chellean and Acheulean industry of Dülük and Kartal'. *Anatolia*, VI, Ankara, 1961.

Bostanci (E.Y.). 'A New Upper Palaeolithic and Mesolithic facies at Belbaşi rock shelter on the mediterranean coast of Anatolia. The Belbaşi industry'. *Belleten*, vol. XXVI, No. 102, 1962.

Boule (M.), Breuil (H.), Licent (E.) and Teilhard (P.). *Le Paléolithique de la Chine*. Paris, 1928.

Howell (F.C.). 'Upper Pleistocene Stratigraphy and Early man in the Levant'. *Proceedings of the American Philosophical Society*, vol. 103, 1959.

Jennings (J.) and Norbeck (E.) eds. *Prehistoric man in the New World*. Chicago, 1964.

Joshi (R.V.). *Pleistocene studies in the Malaprabha Basin*. Deccan College Research Institute, Poona, 1955.

Mayer-Oakes (W.). 'Early Man in the Andes'. *Scientific American*, May, 1963.

Misra (V.N.). 'Palaeolithic culture of Western Rajputana'. *Bulletin of the Deccan College Institute*, vol. 21, n.d.

Movius (H.L.). 'The Lower Palaeolithic cultures of Southern and Eastern Asia'. *Transactions of the American Philosophical Society*, 1948.

Movius (H.L.). 'The Mousterian cave of Teshik-Tash, South Eastern Uzbekistan, Central Asia'. *American school of prehistoric research*, Bull. 17, 1953.

Movius (H.L.). New Palaeolithic sites near Ting-T'sun in the Fen river,

Shansi Province, North China. *Quaternaria*, 111, 1956.

Movius (H.) ed. *Asian Perspectives*. Special Palaeolithic Issue, Hong Kong, 1960.

Neuville (R.). *Le Paléolithique et le Mésolithique du désert de Judée*. Paris, 1951.

Rudenko (S. I.). The Ust' Kanskaya Paleolithic Cave Site, Siberia. *American Antiquity*, vol. 27, October, 1961.

Rust (A.). *Die Höhlenfunde von Jabrud (Syrien)*. Neumünster, 1950.

Sankalia (H. D.). 'Middle Stone Age culture in India and Pakistan'. *Science*, vol. 146, 16 Oct. 1964.

Sen (D.) and Gosh (A. K.). 'Lithic culture-complex in the Pleistocene Sequence of the Narmana Valley, Central India'. *Rivista di Scienze preistoriche*, vol. XVII, 1963.

Solecki (R.). 'Shanidar Cave, a Palaeolithic site in Northern Iraq'. *VIth International Congress on Quaternary, Warsaw, 1961*. Lodz, 1964.

Solecki (R.). 'Shanidar Cave, a Palaeolithic site in Northern Iraq'. *Smithsonian report for 1954*.

Stekelis (M.). 'The Palaeolithic deposits of Jisr Banat-Yaqub'. *Bulletin of the Research Council of Israel*, vol. 9 G, 1960.

Stekelis (M.) and Gilead (D.). 'Ma'ayan Baruckh, a lower Palaeolithic site in Upper Galilee'. *Metqufat Ha-Even*, VIII, 1966.

Sugihara (S.) and Tozawa (M.). 'Pre-Ceramic Age in Japan'. *Acta asiatica*, Tokyo, 1960.

Tindale (N. B.). 'Culture succession in South Eastern Australia from Late Pleistocene to the present'. *Records of the South Australian Museum*, vol. XIII, No 1, 1957.

Tindale (N. B.). 'Ecology of primitive aboriginal man in Australia. Biogeography and Ecology in Australia'. *Monographiae biologicae*, vol. VIII, 1959.

Tindale (N. B.). 'Stone implement making among the Nakako, Ngadadjara and Pitjanjara of the Great Western Desert'. *Records of the South Australian Museum*, vol. 15, No. 1, 1965.

Wormington (M.). *Ancient Man in North America*. Denver Museum of Natural History, 4th edn., 1957.

## Periodicals.

*American Anthropologists.*
*Anthropologie* (l'). Paris.
*Anthropozoikum*, Prague.
*Bulletin de la Société
préhistorique française*, Paris.
*Quartär*, Erlangen.

*Quaternaria*, Rome.
*Proceedings of the Prehistoric
Society*, London.
*Materialy i issledovaniya po
archeologhii SSSR* (and mainly
numbers 39, 59, 79 and 131).

# World University Library

Already published

001 **Eye and Brain**
R. L. Gregory, *Edinburgh*

002 **The Economics of Underdeveloped Countries**
Jagdish Bhagwati, *MIT*

003 **The Left in Europe since 1789**
David Caute, *Oxford*

004 **The World Cities**
Peter Hall, *London*

005 **Chinese Communism**
Robert North, *Stanford*

006 **The Emergence of Greek Democracy**
W. G. Forrest, *Oxford*

007 **The Quest for Absolute Zero**
K. Mendelssohn, *Oxford*

008 **The Biology of Work**
O. G. Edholm, *London*

009 **Palaeolithic Cave Art**
P. J. Ucko and A. Rosenfeld
*London*

010 **Particles and Accelerators**
R. Gouiran, *CERN*

011 **Russian Writers and Society 1825-1904**
Ronald Hingley, *Oxford*

012 **Words and Waves**
A. H. W. Beck, *Cambridge*

013 **Education in the Modern World**
John Vaizey, *Oxford*

014 **The Rise of Toleration**
Henry Kamen, *Warwick*

015 **Art Nouveau**
S. Tschudi Madsen, *Oslo*

016 **The World of an Insect**
Rémy Chauvin, *Strasbourg*

017 **Decisive Forces in World Economics**
J. L. Sampedro, *Madrid*

018 **Development Planning**
Jan Tinbergen, *Rotterdam*

019 **Human Communication**
J. L. Aranguren, *Madrid*

020 **Mathematics Observed**
Hans Freudenthal, *Utrecht*

021 **The Rise of the Working Class**
Jürgen Kuczynski, *Berlin*

022 **The Science of Decision-making**
A. Kaufmann, *Paris*

023 **Chinese Medicine**
P. Huard and M. Wong, *Paris*

024 **Muhammad and the Conquests of Islam**
Francesco Gabrieli, *Rome*

025 **Humanism in the Renaissance**
S. Dresden, *Leyden*

026 **What is Light?**
A. C. S. van Heel and C. H. F. Velzel, *Eindhoven*

027 **Bionics**
Lucien Gérardin, *Paris*

028 **The Age of the Dinosaurs**
Björn Kurtén, *He Isingfors*

029 **Mimicry**
Wolfgang Wickler, *Seewiesen*

031 **Data Study**
J. L. Jolley, *London*